INTERNAL COLLOQUIES

OTHER BOOKS BY I. A. RICHARDS

The Meaning of Meaning (*with* C. K. Ogden)
1923

Principles of Literary Criticism
1925

Practical Criticism
1929

Coleridge on Imagination
1935

The Philosophy of Rhetoric
1936

Interpretation in Teaching
1938

How to Read a Page
1942

Speculative Instruments
1955

"A Leak in the Universe" (*in* Playbook)
1956

Goodbye Earth and Other Poems
1958

The Screens and Other Poems
1960

Tomorrow Morning, Faustus!
1962

So Much Nearer: Essays Toward a World English
1968

Design for Escape
1968

INTERNAL COLLOQUIES

POEMS AND PLAYS OF

I. A. RICHARDS

FURTHER POEMS (1960–1970)

GOODBYE EARTH AND OTHER POEMS

THE SCREENS AND OTHER POEMS

TOMORROW MORNING, FAUSTUS!

JOB'S COMFORTING

HARCOURT BRACE JOVANOVICH, INC.
NEW YORK

"Relaxed Terza Rima" appeared originally in *Poetry*. Other new poems appeared for the first time in *The Harvard Advocate, The New York Review of Books, The New York Times,* and *The Times Literary Supplement*. "Finhaut" is reprinted from the *New Statesman,* London, by permission.

First edition

ISBN 0–15–144635–0
Library of Congress Catalog Card Number: 76–160408
Printed in the United States of America
A B C D E

TO
D.E.P.
NEARING
YET

Titles may reflect, dewdrop wise, the problems of composition. *Internal Colloquies,* I take it, can allude to them all. Around every phrase—behind, on all sides, and ahead—there are other phrases: ready to compete or support, or recklessly bent on having their own way. It is no great leap, hardly even a stride, to assign these rivals and aids, these makers and breakers, various voices. "My name is legion," replied a celebrated colloquist. And the parable of the Sower has its daunting side. So the inclusion of *Tomorrow Morning, Faustus!* and *Job's Comforting* under this title need not surprise. Drama has traditionally claimed (when it cared to) impersonality as compared with Lyric. Exploring readers have not been misled. The various voices overtly distributed in a play may be as distinctly recognizable in what may present itself as straightforward exposition or confession.

"I have several times shown the proprietor the shortest way out of his wood-lot." No doubt Thoreau here is speaking professionally: recalling for a group of surveyors what their art can do. Yet is not the thought itself entitled to spread sail? Who is this Proprietor and how does he stand to his advisers? Who are they and why should he need their advice? Such are the topics of these Internal Colloquies—from "At the Mirror," the first to be written, onward, to whatever Epilogue.

I.A.R.

Cambridge, Massachusetts
December 1970

CONTENTS

THE SCREENS
AND OTHER POEMS
141

FURTHER
POEMS
(1960-1970)

I
RECOGNITIONS

CONDITIONAL

Beckon some cragsman's paradise from the sky,
Heart-beat slows down, lungs halt their heave,
So to descry, conceive
How it was with me when that sport began:
Muscle and nerve wrought for me by the strain.
Fain as of old I feign that yet I can.

Pass by some image of the world's desire,
Eye beam narrows, glance sharpens to discern,
So to attire, adorn
Some visitant from when that hunt began
Whose hardihood now tells me what is vain.
Fain as of old why feign that yet I can?

Butterfly thought, sail gaily through the void,
Seeking your mate, belike - gale-borne astray,
To be destroyed, betray,
Ice-caught, the thoughts from which your life began:
Torn downy wings that will not sail again.
Fain as of old, I feign that yet I can.

Turn the mind then to that
Which being won all's done.
Stable it there
To take that rest as best.
Too many the mind's roads,
Their throngs too beat, too fleet,
Too unaware.
Mind is its bonds
And they'll not break.
       How wake?

Wake! Why, I'm wide awake,
Feel, think as though I know.
Or, is it, knew?
Know, knew it: what I'm not
And what I have to do
Both when and now. But how?
Being beyond my mind
Yet with a bond to keep,
I've both to find
       And sleep.

Out of the ancient flux
Poised here to chart some part,
I note the alternates
Mutual as mates:
The nights and days, and praise
How the clear eye, our sky,
Must cloud and close,
Wear out as sieve;
That others live
       Must die.

Should what I would chart here
Come to seem plain, how vain,
Inept, absurd!
What's it about but doubt?
As if a word
Could be, without
An utterance, heard
Or hearer hear
Save in some subduing
          Of din.

What a word means who'ld say
Will new words choose and use;
What these in turn may mean
Invities a new to-do.
And so on. . .please.
But when the sense is seen,
What then has been,
What's clear in that serene,
What seeing is
          Who sees?

To say now what I know
About my send and end:
Rudder'd I am and sail'd,
Can set a course, enforce,
Amend, subvert, rebel.
That's mutiny, for we
Life-long are all at sea;
Captaining it
As our ghostly crew
          See fit.

Not, by a sight, by chance.
As we begin there's in
Us, unconceived, our plan;
We've each our bent; are sent
To show what comes of that;
In such self-government must ask,

7

Cell ask of cell, "What's well?"
But to pursue
　　　Our task.

Its end? What but to probe:
Record, prepare, bear, share. . .
That the design may grow
Worth even its cost.
The lost, they show
Us what we're for.
We but relay. What more?
What further care?
　　　You say.

"My Mind to me a kingdom is."
   But I,
   Whatever is named Thereby,
     Am not its King
     - No, that there's no mistaking -
But one of its agencies.

"The proper study of mankind"
   Could be
   This proper realm to free
     By ridding it,
     Day by hour by minute,
Of what deforms a mind.

Be then dissolved this Parliament
   That long
   Where it did not belong
     Did this neglect.
     But now, how to elect
Some fitting government?

Set Parties up. Prepare the lists.
   Now find
   Within your million'd mind
     A loyalty
     A price and penalty
That's binding and persists.

Who'll take to heart this parable?
  With all
  It has that can appal:
    Injustices
    And Fate's felinities
In the incalculable?

Dare you now ride Dictator-wise?
  (Except
  The Ruler you accept
    Be the Unknown?)
    And have then on the Throne
But passions in disguise?

New States their single-parties win
  And who
  Won't do as they're told to do
    In prison wait,
    While grief and fear and hate
Grow, till the war begin.

To rule oneself's the dream of dreams.
  "Be free!"
  Heartbreaking then to see
    Liberty won
    Lost, the great work undone,
Real men the prey of schemes.

Within as between our fluctuant minds
  The oppressed
  Set up self-poisonings in the rest.
    To represent's
    The sanity of governments.
As the sick tyrant finds.

None the less, Rule's required.
    If I
    Fit government can't supply,
       What other plan
       Holds out more hope we can
Live as we have desired?

A dual plan: like man and wife;
    Two sets
    Of promises and debts;
       Two gangs of eyes
       Watching for *gaffes* and lies;
Domesticating strife.

Such Troths need Truth, as curb and lead;
    Need still,
    Indeed, whatever will
       Folly gainsay
       As, vyingly, they
Make as they may Godspeed.

Out then with Ideologies
    For States,
    As for a mind's inmates.
       For the communal
       And individual
This nobler way there is.

PLUPERFECT PROGRESSIVE

Thoughts on Contemporary Sculpture

Who had been thinking it had reached an end. . .
Who had been hoping it would but go on. . .
Who'd been supposing there'd be nothing more. . .

I

Honor we and console the pioneer
So unillusioned, so unreconciled,
Who turned from what went on,
Tuned a deaf ear,
Grew wild;

Who had been thinking it had reached an end,
Thinking there would be nothing else to come,
Nothing but "gas and gaiters."
As well be dumb!
Attend:

Tired of the actual, the articulate,
The formed and uttered, clear, explicit Word;
Tired out with trying for it. . .
One who had heard
Ululate

A homeless, formless, soulless ghost of being
(Not to be caught, to be invoked in vain)
Bought it by turning in.
All in, on pain
Of seeing

Your own pet fancies only, fat or thin
Or moderate as your reducer's chart.
How now? Aha! That's that:
A new New Art
Within.

They are underground, the currents we obey.
Winds of the spirit? Strainings in the field,
Shifting beyond our guessing.
And we and they
Must yield,

Who'd been supposing there'd be nothing more,
Suddenly sidling slantwise from the strain
In the unthought-of vein.
Worldquake again.
Encore!

III

The arrogant at heart, timid without,
Their converse cousins, fearful, therefore bold,
Have the appetitive eye;
Soon see what's sold:
Smart doubt.

So smart it has promoters on the "If?!"
- These formulae are generalized in a wink,
Académicized right off.
"What would you think?"
"Terrif!"

Ripe now for posters, knick-knacks, shop
Décor - "what the Committee 'ull approve.
Raise the site's value . . ."
"Right! In the groove!
On top!"

Customers worrying over what they ought
To want - new opened wide the slot -
Light-heartedly aghast,
Buy it for what
Its NOT.

IV

Pity though those sand-agonists adroit
Led off so into nowhere. Period.
Hard though take to heart
For docile squad
Or poet.

Who had been hoping it would but go on . . .
Forever finding the new line cut again,
Self-sealed, self-turned off,
Abruptly gone,
Self-slain.

How wait now till the Dynasties return?
O, pre-dynastic primitives by choice,
What's history for? Who'd been
Harkening its voice
Might learn.

Flying this low, below that river bed
    There shows another, another under that,
    Palimpsest meanderings outspread.

Horizon-wide, the piedmont falls so flat
    The streams can wander - freely, we might say.
    Cut where they will, spill over, twine and plait,

Explore, essay, renege, revert or play
    What ox-bow games they please; lick at a bank,
    Silt up a channel; anyway, have their way.

Not so at all. We've something else to thank!
    All streams in sight in parallel have told
    A common story; it was the West that sank

Tilting all beds together; each stream rolled
    The way it had to. East and West in turn
    Sway - see-saw - up and down. All flow's controlled.

The whole world wiggles; wriggle we must and learn
    How the earthwave within us bulges by,
    Troughs us or hoists, whichever way we yearn.

Not harsh or crabbed, as dull schools imply,
    But queer beyond all that, we may discern,
    Beyond our like or loathing, grin or sigh,

    How daunting is divine autonomy.

No heron, swung
Squint-eyed
Above its tide,
Full-strung
To dart,
Is more alert:
    Stir in a reed,
    Horizon head,
    Flaw in the flood. . .
At once, wide wings abroad
He's up
Away.
Who prey are prey.

So I
Minding my step
And sky,
Where any air
Can scare me from
My nearer aim;
Where the unknown
    Controls the scene
    Stages the show,
    The persons too. . .
Writes all anew
To ask me: Who
The playwright is?
Whose prey are you?
What sort of game
With thing or thought
Could be your own?

What 'gator now
    Below, behind. . .
    Within your mind. . .
Some predator,
Shadow of harm,
With what swift fright
Shakes you to flight,
Makes you let swim
The fish in sight,
Flap off, alight
From brief survey
Elsewhere; there stay
While it's your whim
Or till some
Fresh alarm?

Here on this strand,
With what would do
Well within thrust,
You wait. You trust.
May your fish too
Be trustful! And
May those who wait
For you!
This is your Fate:
Not soon or late,
But ever;
Minute by minute
In it.

II
CONJECTURES

Am I not the original Ball
Tossed into Court to call
     The players to their Game:
Those tireless Players who
Do what they have to do
     That's never twice the same?

That Ball, those Players, that Court are all a Mask:
Each for the rest a token. Should you ask
     What each apart is, answer could be none.
No stroke without a striker, Ball and aim,
Opponent, ambience, audience and the Game
     Whose Rules determine who has lost, who won.

That old Game had a Rule
Made it a fine school
     For a clever Player;
The loser more than lost,
Lost out and, lost, was lost,
     Was slain, not Slayer.

And I, the Ball,
Miming the All,
Am still the Players there,
Bounce in their bounds,
Run with their sweat and share
The spin of their despair.

. . .and placed him on the stone. . .and opened his breast. . .
and took out the heart and threw it at the feet of the statue. . .

—*Sahagún*

Serene
Amid the Coils
That hold and mold us all:
The fanged enfolding Wall
That our own toils
Convene,

On dust
My left I set
My right hand near my Heart:
An Offering from the start
That beats on yet
And must.

The Sign
My brow must wear:
The Feathered Serpent's Mask,
Lays upon me this task,
This charge I bear
As mine.

As stone:
As cold, as keen,
As the Obsidian Knife,
I free a Heart from life.
May what this mean
Atone!

And you,
Too, Brother Priest,

Hand too upon your Heart,
Know, as you play this Part,
The Heart released
Your own.

Bear with these models for the musing Self:
A pair of hands a-fumble out of sight
Matching and fitting its intangibles,
Ready enough to stick them on the Shelf.

Captain to Mate: "Mate tell us a story!"
And duly then the Mate begins his tale:
"A Gentle Knight was pricking on the plaine
To slay a Dragon and to win him glory. . ."

Higher the hills, grimmer the gruesome way,
And lit like Hell's own throat the livid sky.
Between its Fangs into the Vale we rode
Into the rumours of our common day.

That Pair of Hands, that Captain and his Mate,
That quested Worm whose wame's become our World,
Rider and Rocinante: all these are one.
To find none but such models is our Fate.

THEODICY

An Internal Colloquy

Of that place above the heavens no earthly poet has yet
well sung nor ever will. . . There true being lives: color-
less, shapeless, untouchable; it is seen only by the mind,
the soul's pilot, and all true knowledge is of that. . . And
therefore it is just that only the mind of the philosopher
has wings, being ever, as best it may, in communion
through memory with those things communion with which
makes a god divine.

—Phaedrus, 247–249

> Whence then cometh Wisdom?
> And where is the place of understanding?
> *—Job* 28:20

LUCIFER: Well-omened, out beyond
          Almost this laser's throw,
  Can you respond?

FAUSTUS: Light-bringer, can you know
  What power of man am I
      Who lightless go?

LUCIFER: Fleetingly you sweep by,
          Your generations those
  Who live and die;
          Yet do you Time compose;
  So to the Everliving
          You disclose
  What comes of our conceiving,
          Without you vainer far

Our Timeless sieving,
Than your wild dash and jar
That the world-aim advances
Or might debar.

FAUSTUS: Ah, Lord of all mischances!
Well do you speak of them:
The traitorous stances
From which our failures stem,
Our dread derelictions
Beyond requiem.

LUCIFER: You weigh not your afflictions.
Let us now sort and rate
Our jurisdictions.

FAUSTUS: A stain of foam, I wait
On the sway of gain and loss;
Refluent in gait,
Among my waves must toss;
While you, unstirred by Time,
Gaze still across
The threat, the Fall, the climb,
The strokes, the dizzyings of despair,
Of change, of chime.

LUCIFER: Time-free, our single care,
Through disguisings and estrangings,
That our lines bide where
We set them and their rangings
E'er Time might dare
Its sly exchangings.
Though titled Prince of the Air
(Hearest thou the sound thereof,
Born of the spirit thou?),
Adversary as well,
Alert where'er,
And famous Lord of Hell,

The Tempter at the Tree;
    Not all they tell
Is truth, truth that may be
    In your due Time set out.
In truth, though we
    So several seem without,
Within we almost blend
    Bout after bout.
    (As Jacob at his Jabbok ford,
    Wrestling that Lord.)
You upon me depend;
    I on you: now new discerned
Each other's End.

FAUSTUS: Hardly and slow we have learned
Feared, tortured, despised,
    Otherward yearned;
I in each thought apprized
    But by some intuition
By you devised,
    By you upheld; your vision
The ray behind my sight
    My Precognition!

LUCIFER: And you, o rueful Knight
    In your triumphs and undoings
Proof of our sleight.
    Not that by such accruings
New constellations show;
    In your reviewings. . .

FAUSTUS: What's known we come to know
    More duly. So we pray.

LUCIFER: It has been so.

FAUSTUS: (The mansions are yours;
              The rueings in their ruins, ours.)
          Yet, Adversary, say
          What came to that good servant, Job,
              As you went your way?

LUCIFER: "Going to and fro on the globe,
              And up and down on it?"
          I sent a probe.

FAUSTUS: "Does Job fear God for naught?"

LUCIFER: It proved so. But those friends!
              (So wide astray,
                  Squinting at pay.)

FAUSTUS: Then came the poet. . .

LUCIFER: Writing what no one comprehends:
              Another story. Job held true.

FAUSTUS: Those strange amends.

LUCIFER: Who then could feel as you?
          After his griefs he had
              For a thousand head, two.

FAUSTUS: (And after all those slaughters
                  Yet fairer daughters.)
          Amends aren't payment, would you add?

LUCIFER: Where all is all its own reward,
          For good and bad.

FAUSTUS: What then of the exiling Sword,
          The loss of Paradise,
              Does that accord?

LUCIFER: Were they before so wise?
                    Would you give up your sight
            For innocent eyes?
                    How cleave off wrong from right?
            Or evil clear from good?
                    Or depth from height?
                    (Whoever this denies,
                        Ask how man came about.)

FAUSTUS: You too, O Everliving,
                    Thus Timelessly devout,
            Whence came your Being?

LUCIFER: From that prime journeying out
            And lifting up our Seeing
            To WISDOM's hardihood,
                    Source too of doubt.

FAUSTUS: Whoever'ld gainsay could
                    Not care for comprehension.
            Unundersood
                    The heart-beat holding tension
            Serving the breath of life
                    In all invention.
            Discovery's not strife
                    Though so possessives dream,
                    Fondling the knife.

LUCIFER: Possessives so possessed, redeem
            Who can! Their poison's fear.
                    Wide off their beam
            They drift who'ld hope to hear
                    Some final word or see
            Entirety clear.

FAUSTUS: Your Role ever to be
            For any Absolute Being
                    The Adversary.

LUCIFER: My Call, my Charge, to bring
                  The denied side before
          The doting King.
                  Utopias of whatsoever colour
          What's wrong with them to tell
                  As counsellor.

FAUSTUS: With first, that Heaven whence you fell.

LUCIFER: It and its dummy Despot.

FAUSTUS: And what of Hell?

LUCIFER: The image of men's hate
          As He, Hell's Maker,
                  Their fear of fate.

FAUSTUS: No War in Heaven, dream-breaker?

LUCIFER: No war. Why wars at all,
          Awaker?

FAUSTUS: But why so horrible
          A dream, Utopianist!
                  It can appal.

LUCIFER: It does. Yet you persist.
                  Truth can cut through its way
          For a Platonist.

FAUSTUS: A Satanist, you should say,
          You proto-Socrates.

LUCIFER: You're civil.
                  Be it as may,
          You are at a conversable level,
                  Much learnt since Marlowe's man.
          Dull ass - to the Devil!

FAUSTUS: To others too: the greedy charlatan.
        We're grateful for your word of praise
           Who do what we can.

LUCIFER: And yet I marvel. That such arrays
           Of talents are so wasted
     Should more amaze.

FAUSTUS: Alas! Who have tasted
        Careers of intellect put them first,
           However enlisted.
        The task of shielding from the worst
           Stands low or last for those.
        They might be cursed.

LUCIFER: Surely they are. Who chose,
     The options clear at the test,
           Pays what he owes.

FAUSTUS: Justice still. And, for the rest,
           Why, any distraction
     A welcome guest,
           Not least the heady sands of faction
     Will more than serve their turn:
           Elusive action!
     And thus, collectively, we earn
           What's coming to us: TV'd
     Beyond concern.

LUCIFER: T-V: far-sighted.

FAUSTUS: We'll concede
     It shows things up. Though farther sight
           Is not our need. . .

LUCIFER: True insight is. Through the contrite,
           Self-knowing, unaccusing eye
     There shines a light
           Dissolving its own lie.

FAUSTUS: And who wins that wins free.
                     Not his, his life - being conned
             But by the WHY.

LUCIFER: May the event,
                     Battle beyond,
             Be our Theodicy!

I

Field Theory

The gravitation and the filial bond
—*The Prelude*

Mind upon mind depends
   And my inertia
     My mass, my me
     Should simply be
   The pull of all who were
To this lone knot its friends.

If mind is all its bonds,
   I who invite you now
     Am mine, as you
     Are yours: must do
   As they may sway. That's how
World to world corresponds.

What *there* or *here* in this,
   Or *then* or *now,* may be
     Lapses, redounds;
     We need no grounds
   So mutually
We punctuate the abyss.

The Vale

A spacious valley in the kingdom of Amhara, surrounded
on every side by mountains, of which the summits overhang
the middle part.

—*The History of Rasselas*

Eye-perpendicular
   These cliffs;
   Tissue of *but*s and *if*s,
Of let and bar.

Whose crests surround and seal
   This Vale
   In which we hope and fail,
Despair and heal.

Sleek slabs that lean and tilt
   And rear,
   On which to balance fear
And pride and guilt,

And learn there's no way through,
   No out,
   Whatever a stubborn doubt
May set us to

Up here with peg and sling.
   Who try
   The spider's way rely
On the hammer's ring;

Listen themselves secure,
   Until
   Will, over-reaching skill,
Its end endure.

Built me up duly
To seem what I should:
Guide for all comers;
Stoneman beyond
Winters and summers,
Cannot and could;
Steadfast, in bond,
Shafted secure,
With a crest of bright quartz
To sharpen the lure.

Links in a chain
Should stonemen be,
Each man again
His next men see
Upholding plain
Joint guarantee
For one bent whither
And him bound thence
And you won hither
None may know whence:
Servants, escorts,
Companions, defence.

Not stand alone
Only its own
Answerless stone.

Knowing no neighbour,
Distant or near,
Sharing no labour;
Dutyless here.

Though as his duty,
As for that sent,
In that spent,
Bearing the blame,
But as his duty
One came,
Built me up truly,
Built me
And went.

Built me up duly
To seem. . .

III
BALLAD PLAYS

JACOB: Go, servants, seek Lord Esau out
           High in the land of Seir,
     "Let now Lord Esau know no doubt
           If Jacob now draw near."

     And further say: "These twenty years
           In Laban's house he stayed
     For gain to calm Lord Esau's fears;
           And be no more afraid.

     And oxen, asses, rams and ewes
           He has for thy delight,
     And sends us now to bear this news. . .
           To find grace in thy sight."

NARRATOR: To Esau came these servants then
           Bowing unto the ground:
ESAU: "Whose?"
SERVANTS: "Thy servant Jacob's men."
NARRATOR: Then Esau grimly frowned.

ESAU: "Go tell that double-crossing ape,
           That birthright-buying cat,
     This next time he will not escape."
NARRATOR: And as he spake he spat.

ESAU: "Pottage, yes and savoury meat,
           The hairy neck and hands!
     Go tell that smoothy let his feet
           Not step into my lands.

Or blessings shall he get from me
    The blessings of the sword,
For him and his.   Sands of the sea!
    Beyond the eddying ford!"

NARRATOR: So sped, those servants came again
    Saying:
SERVANTS: "Here Esau comes
And with him come four hundred men
    With spears and swords and drums."

NARRATOR: Then greatly Jacob grew afraid
    Lest Esau from his wild
Come down and slaughter man and maid,
    The mother with the child.

To appease such brotherly amity
    Two hundred ewes and rams,
Two hundred goats, both he- and she-,
    And camel colts and dams

He gave into his servants' hands
    To go forth, drove by drove,
Grazing across Lord Esau's lands
    To be his luck and trove,

And straitly charged each servant now:
JACOB: "When Esau meeteth thee,
And asketh: 'Whence and whose art thou?'
    Thus shall thine answer be:

'Thy servant Jacob's are we all
    - May we be to thy mind! -
And others follow at thy call,
    And he, he comes behind.' "

RACHEL: Help us, O Teraphim I stole,
    When we bow before this Lord!
JACOB: O FEAR of Isaac, may this toll
    Save *Joseph* from the sword!

40

O FEAR, deliver even me
    From my brother's angry hands!
Surely, Thou saids't, shall thy seed be
    As the sea's unnumbered sands.

NARRATOR: So flock by flock his presents passed,
    Well-spaced, across the ford;
Then wives and offspring, Joseph last,
    To shield him from the sword.

And Jacob stayed and was alone
    Before the ford that night.
JACOB: What more have I that is my own
    To give or hold by right?

THE EL: Thyself.
JACOB: And what art thou?
THE EL: Thyself.
JACOB: Wrestle thou then with me!
THE EL: Myself to overcome Myself
    Will wrestle here with thee.

JACOB: What art thou but this eddying ford
    By which I sent across,
To save me from my brother's sword,
    My winnings and my loss.

THE EL: And thou too art this eddying ford
    By which were sent across
To save thee from thy brother's sword:
    Those winnings and that loss.

JACOB: Long is this night we wrestle out,
    Yet dayspring draweth nigh,
Foul-handled though I be this bout
    In the hollow of my thigh.

THE EL:	Let go! Day breaketh on the sky!
	Day breaketh! Let me go!
JACOB:	Yet shalt thou bless me from on high
	Or e'er I let thee go.

THE EL:	By what name?
JACOB:	Jacob.
THE EL:	Now be given
	Thy new name Israel:
	God striveth. Who with God hath striven
	O'er men shall he prevail.

JACOB:	And thy name? Thine? I pray thee, thine?
THE EL:	Why dare'st thou ask my name?
	Yet do I bless thee. And the sign
	Shall this be: thou art lame.

NARRATOR:	And Jacob called by name the place
	Peniel: *The Face of God.*
JACOB:	For here have I seen God face to face
	Yet onward yet I plod.

NARRATOR:	And lifting up his eyes he saw,
	As he limped along again,
	Under the risen sun, Esau
	And his four-hundred men.

POSADA

For reading by groups, during the ten days before Christmas. Through this period, it is the custom in Oaxaca, Mexico, for friends to pay evening calls upon one another. They expect to have to knock loud and long before they are admitted. They are enacting Joseph's harrowing appeals.

Around the churches at sundown companies of clamant, excited children batter on firmly closed doors; within, companies of equally clamant children refuse them admittance. All the doors of the church are besieged in turn by the chanting procession. Finally, there is a grand climax. All doors are opened and there is candy galore for all.

This little play tries to combine after-sunset arrivals at many village inns in remote desert landscapes with the Pre-Christmas drama.

MARY: Go Joseph knock! O knock again!
              Again knock on the Door!

SATAN: That this all-labouring world of pain
              Need travel on no more.

GABRIEL: That what will be may be
              And what must be can be
              That what could be should be.

MARY: Yet, yet, again! Knock on again!
              Again knock on the Door!

SATAN: That this nigh-foundering race of men
              Learn what the sword is for.

JOSEPH: So I, despairing, hammer on my heart.
              O open, open wide and let blow in
              The unsparing Word that chose me for this part,
              Filling this void that's hunger and that's sin.

PORTER: Knock at this hour! Be off, you there!
　　　　　Why should we find you room!
　　　No opening now, for pay nor prayer.
　　　　　Think you're the crack of doom!

　　　They come by day the folk that we let in
　　　　　To take their ease, for light and food and sleep.
　　　This Door won't open now for all your din.
　　　　　An Inn's an Inn and not a fortress keep.

INNKEEPER: This night's not like another night.
　　　　　Some THING's abroad I doubt.
　　　My porter there is in the right
　　　　　To keep these vagrants out.

GUEST IN
THE INN: Slow and cold, dust blowing all the way:
　　　　　Wind-burn parched and foot and saddle sore.
　　　A ruinous place but still a place to stay.
　　　　　What's all that argie-bargie at the Door?

ANOTHER
GUEST: Snug here! Let's hope those batterings at the Door
　　　　　Don't mean the You Know Who have caught
　　　　　　us up!
　　　I had as lief not fight it out once more.
　　　　　Meanwhile we may as well fill up the cup.

SERVING
WENCH: A pinchy lot to serve their meat and drink,
　　　　　Smile at, be saucy with - and sometimes
　　　　　　more:
　　　At beck and call to any nod or wink.
　　　　　Ah, that young lad so haggard at the Door.

ANOTHER
GUEST: Good pickings maybe. No pig in a poke.
　　　　　Some chance, at least, to see which of them's
　　　　　　which.
　　　Who wants to waste his talents on the broke?
　　　　　So here's our bumper toast: "God Save the
　　　　　　Rich!"

44

ANOTHER
GUEST: It's just as well we left the pearls behind.
Don't too much like the looks of some of these.
Better not seem to have it on your mind.
These gentry's style in arguing isn't "Please!"

ANOTHER
GUEST: Stoney the waste and blinding chill the wind,
Secretive and hid the passers-by.
Men get more talkative when they have dined
Grow less inclined to take you for a spy.

JOSEPH: What Inn is this? So pitiless its Door,
It will not hark or heed
It will not hear however I implore
It will not even let me show the Need.

O more than life to me, so not my life;
Why you, all this on you be laid,
O my betrothed, my partner not my wife?
What doom is this set on an honest maid?

FIRST
NEIGHBOUR: She looks too good to be in such a plight.
Demure yet proud.   Uppish, no doubt.
But now she comes to learn what serves her right:
In such a night as this to be shut out!

SECOND
NEIGHBOUR: Nothing but riff-raff, flotsam of the Ways.
Improvident and feckless are the poor!
Without the wit even to count the days!
Then go and knock on any decent door!

DONKEY: Hee-haw!   See-saw!   She's had her fun and fling!
And now it's all caught up with her at last,
She must have been the doxy of a King;
Not that poor chap so helpless and aghast.

SATAN: Here is my cue to play the Morning Star!
Too big she is to weather out the night.
I'll show them where the hay and manger are.
Follow me now, all Glory and all Might.

GABRIEL: Helpful as ever the Adversary is,
    Alert to forward what he calls his plan.
The very first to think he knows what's his,
    Acting his part out between God and man.

That what will be may be
And what must be can be
That what could be should be.

IV
MOODS AND TENSES

PRESENT INTERROGATIVE, IMPERATIVE, INDICATIVE, DECLARATIVE

What *now?*   Contain
Your futuring glance;
Restrain
Your probings of the realm of
    chance.

This *now*.   Not then!
Then's all conjecturing.
Hold in,
Hold down that gambler's sallying?

Be *now* - remark
The voice below your breath:
Our Ark,
Only overt antagonist of death.

For, *now* - between
What's gone and what's ahead:
The mean
Of all - says all that can be said.

Says all.   And should
Some sequent *now* ask: "What?"
This should
Reply: "Hark! And deny me not!"

Would I had!
Would I had seen!
Would I had said. . .
Would that I'd. . . done. . .

The sparrows peck and scuffle there.
An ant hies on
Under my empty stare.

Would that I were. . .
Would I were gone!

Look forward lightly. No news ever yet
Could be as good or bad as it appear.
Don't cross the sundering flood before it's here,
Getting all set to meet what mayn't be met.

It's coming; yes, of course. But what will come?
What no one knows - so, ignorance, be still.
Go make your bed and glance up at the hill.
The hill's the whence, although the hope be mum.

Making the bed, what fleeting tremor's shed,
As 'twere an echo of an inner laughter;
A scent, fore-sending, of a follow-after?
Look forward lightly yet and make your bed.

If it were so,
If so it were,
Actually so;
Being no bare
Matter-of-fact,
No here or there,
No: being a sheer
Being, an act -
Should we not care?

O, an it were so,
So, an it were,
Unutterably so:
Being our bare
Matter, our fact,
Our hope-shot despair,
Our lack and the lacked,
Our utterance, our pact,
Our outcome, our prayer.

Seeing it so,
No 'as it were';
Utterly so:
Seeing it clear,
Sheerly a fact,
Here and not there,
Nearer than fear,
Perfect, exact -
Now we can care.

V
MISCELLANY

FOR THE 50TH BIRTHDAY OF
ROBERT LOWELL

Out of our 'teens, from woes a-plenty,
It seemed a sound step: to be twenty.

By thirty, O the case was plain:
We'd never be so good again.

At forty, as we well recall,
We'd had it, and we'd said it, all.

But, once you've climbed on up to fifty
Of joys it's idle to be thrifty;

The world is yours, indeed your oyster:
Year after year, bigger and moister.

A welcome age this day began.
Hail, demi-centenarian!

With this I end my madrigal
Happy returns be yours, dear Cal!

FOR THE 99TH BIRTHDAY OF
CONRAD AIKEN

Four years and four decades ago
Your notice taught me what I'ld owe
To one who, an acknowledged Prince,
Has guided critics ever since.
No trifling work. Now that you're 80,
However others may grow pratey,
Your wit's as quick, as fresh, as weighty.
A wonder this to more than laity
To all a cause for joy and gaiety.
Alas! There's no nice rime for 90
Except some brash young word like "pinty."
And should we charge right on to an 100,
You'ld be saying: "Someone'd blund'red."

CONFIDENCES

"Everything is what it is and not another thing."
So Bishop Butler happily secure.

"Everything is where it is, afoot or on the wing."
So sing the hunters, not a bit as sure.

"Everything is where and when it fling its uttering."
So Sirius, flourishing its battledore.

Under-worry one:
What's done is done;
Leave ill alone!

Weary wonder two:
What could I do
Hearing them all:
Call against call?

Why, I could weep!

On-coming trouble three:
Hamlet's, Cuchulain's sea.

Reap as I've sown?

Throw up the sponge?

Before it fall
Into what sweet deep
Waters of sleep
Do I plunge

Strain ear
Strain eye
Strain brain
Until appear:
   Something
   To steer
   By.

Something,
New or old,
Certain to hold:
   Something
   To cling
   To.

O shame
Forbid!

Your clue
Your cue:
Firm word
Sure heard,
Clear view;
That vow
You now
So do
Disdain,
You did,
You, you,
Impose.
You chose.

All those
Dubieties,
Velleities:
Our verities,
Our sureties,
They came,
They too,
From you.

FACULTY MEETING

(Lord Faustus, considering his Pact,
reviews some of the Subjects)

Studies and Sciences, the more they're pure:
Pure Poetry, Art for its own sake. . .all the rest,
Have - every several one of them - its Muse,
Guardian, Familiar, Genius. . . They're possessed
By Daimons not unlike those I endure.

Tutelaries, capable, devout,
Indeed devoted, wholly given up,
Envious, self-seeking, power-mad. . .
Sly-soul'd fanatics; whoever'ld sup
With any, long tho' the spoon, look out!

My mathematical allies would explain
Me and my notions gaily into functions,
Values (God save the word), choice primitives
And tacit constants; then, with no compunctions,
Flush all the saving residue down the drain.

Maths are to physics as schemata to Deed:
They had to try their Bomb out that grave day.
"So, doubly seconded with will and power,
Must make perforce an universal prey"?
"Wolf! Wolf!" now well worn out. What use to plead?

What pleas can weigh with those caught in that tissue?
Who have to climb that high, they have to win:
Must smile, laugh, frown, speak so - then think
With what's left over. Once they're *in*
The web's own owner takes care of the issue.

Politics, old Spinner, change your skin,
As variously as suits you, you don't change.
No less than Maths or Physics you immure
Your adepts in a world they so arrange
No brash outsiders may come butting in.

So with all crafts - Psychology not least,
Arts too, when artful; even Philosophy,
Become a bag of tricks, a line of talk,
A set of games with games, a vanity
Dodging the duty - not the dues - of priest.

Theology, fair abdicated Queen,
Quean still, Lear's Godmother, Beatrice of the slum,
Proclaiming now that nothing she can say
Says more than "Nothing!" Yet you're not so dumb
Who give away yet hold the old desmesne.

RELAXED TERZA RIMA

For Marianne Moore

On taking a more rational order of being

Say to her, "Do,"
As is your wont,
You. Who are you?

What do you want
Clipping away
With "do" and with "don't,"
With "can" and with "can't,"
"Will you" and "won't"?

Psyche, we say,
Feminine, she.
She? Who is she,
Standing at bay,
When we say to her "shan't"?

On taking on?
"On" means *about*
And *about to,* too,
Having so done,
And *having to do,*
As well as, no doubt,
That being won!

More rational, yes,
But who's to choose?
Is it a dress
Psyche must wear,
Trying it on,
Letting it out,
Taking it in?

Try out a guess
At what "it" 's at there,
Neat as a pin,
Lip-loads of 'em
Constrain a grin.

Trying what on?
A season's wear?
Letting what out?
Not only "where?"
Taking who in?

So with orderliness.
None would condemn
What the deceptious
Do with a hem.

Conscientious
Folk, though, claim
That to look alright
Isn't all our aim;
That shining bright
Isn't the same,
As yet, for us,
As being alight
With the gem-like flame;
That we are not yet quite
Without use for shame.
Our thanks to them;
No animus.

Where are you going to, my witty maid,
    And, what may your true name be?
Psyche's my name, kind sir, she said,
    Curtseying comelily.

Psyche, you know what risks you run
    Here all alone, said he.
Risks all alone, gay sir, there are none.
    Risks come from company.

Goddess you must be, Psyche dear,
    For beast you could never be.
And Aristotle has made it clear
    You've no other choice, said he.

One who would live to herself alone,
    And a beauty especially,
Must, it has often enough been shown,
    Be a brute or a deity.

Why yet, fond sir, try what you will,
    Alone I would ever be,
My own, my strange, companion still,
    Undesolatedly.

Poor Belial, were you still a soul,
    Or a soul could you ever see,
You'ld know why all who seek their goal
    Still journey lonelily.

65

Here where the snow drifts shrink,
High upon Summer's brink
    Our station is;
Our tassel heads we thrust
Up through the icy crust.

Through Winter's full defeat
We signaled his retreat,
    Our out-going his;
For when his snows are gone
Not long we linger on.

Who were the first to bring
Our witness to those Spring
    Festivities
Hear through these parching days
Breeze echoes of that praise.

FINHAUT

(Highest point on the railway over from Martigny
to the French frontier at Le Châtelard.)

An ominous name? Could be:
These gyring rails must mount no higher,
Firmly descend into another country.

Their duty's done. What though
Across the numinous gulf uprear
Sheer spires and sunlit snow;

Along this ravining brink
Our wheels will wind their squeal;
Tunnel to trestle to tunnel blink

On down, past footways to
Known heights now out of reach;
To this pass come, and through:

Who, sixty-odd years ago,
Happened here first to lift
My young mere eyes to snow.

Not much left now to prize: in gait,
In posture, contour, poise to rate:
Uncouthenings so thick of late
Slim the chance that they'll abate
While what's ensuing we await.
Ah well! Why cavil at one's fate?
   In Arcady the limbs are straight.

Nor much more scope for articulate
Comparings of the great with great;
And filterings out of scorn and hate;
Compassionate eyeing of the counterfeit.
Frustration's still our true estate.
Ah well! Why quarrel with the date?
   In Arcady ideals create.

No Court, no Rules, no Net,
No Score; and yet
    Paradigm to outreach
    Whatever Theory of Games may teach:
Von Neumann, Wittgenstein. . .
In fine,
    Non-plus'd,
    Sarcophagus'd;
Their sallies
Irrelevant to these rallies.

No winning-losing in this Game
Whose players play with so remote an aim
    It might well move the World.
    These feather'd corks uptwirl'd
Figure such courses
They might be Plato's horses
    Or Cave folk led,
    Blow sped,
Toward the Sun,
But then
Doom'd to descend again,
    To be or not
        Returned.

Two players there,
Ego and *alter,* bear
    Each other's quirks
    And shirks
Faults
And assaults

With bonhommie
Or irony,
This being a colloquy
In which each seeks reply;
Any: whose return,
Flippant or stern,
Maintains their tie.

For *alter* as his due
Requires that we renew
Inconsequential strife;
As I do too
It being Our Life.
Yet while we feint this out,
In mutual doubt,
Jointly we sustain
The incessant rain
Of no such feathery freight,
Jointly must generate
Reply
To whatsoever might untie
One knot of those whereby
We death defy.

These mortal darts repelled,
That rallying upheld,
We've still
The ventures of our will:
What we should do?
Who
Be?
Who see
As our Opponent there?
Why care?
How yearn?
What fate
As our return
Await,

Who know our hopes for shuttles too,
Turn-turtling at their crests of flight?

And you? Whose battledores are you
    Who help us through
    This plight?

GOODBYE
EARTH
AND
OTHER
POEMS

TO
D.E.P.
ALONG
THE
RIDGE

PROEM

The temptation to the poet to try to tell his readers how his lines may best be read must often be considerable. But to a writer much of whose life has been passed in studying the *difficulties* poems present to even very well-qualified readers the itch to lend a helping word becomes acute. It is notable, however, that poets have rarely offered explanations—as if to be mysterious and unforthcoming about his work were a part of the poet's role. Those who have departed from it have felt the need of disguise. Edgar Allan Poe, for example, may profess to be contributing to the Philosophy (or Linguistics, as we might now say) of Composition, but is quick to slight what he has to reveal by presenting it as material for "a magazine paper":

I have often thought how interesting a magazine paper might be written by an author who would—that is to say who could—detail, step by step, the processes by which one of his compositions attained its ultimate point of completion. Why such a paper has never been given to the world, I am much at a loss to say; but perhaps the authorial vanity has had more to do with the omission than any other cause. Most authors—poets in especial—prefer having it understood that they compose by a species of fine frenzy—an ecstatic intuition; and would positively shudder at letting the public take a peep behind the scenes at the elaborate and vacillating crudities of thought, at the true purposes seized only at the last moment, at the innumerable glimpses of idea that arrived not at the maturity of full view, at the fully matured fancies discarded in despair as unmanageable, at the cautious selections and rejections, at the painful erasures and interpolations—in a word at the wheels and pinions. . . .

These fine promises have disappointed many. As the revelation is unfolded we are accorded no such peep *behind* the scenes, only more and more grandiose scenery. It is as though Poe's nerve failed him, if indeed he ever intended more than an ingenious puff for *The Raven*. We may suspect, with sympathy,

75

that he may have cared too much for admiration, have suffered from "the authorial vanity" too much himself, to be able to publish a regardless and exact account of his composition.

But there is great if rare example, surely, for explaining poems along with presenting them: Dante's glosses in *La Vita Nuova* occur to me (as other instances may to others). I recall that when I first read them, as a schoolboy, poem and gloss seemed to be about equally matched for obscurity. They did, however, reflect provoking lights upon one another. And it seemed, and still seems, reassuring and confirming to the exploring mind that there should be (for some sorts of poetry, at least) a structure capable of an exposition in ordered, articulate prose, whether supplied by the poet or to be worked out by his reader; whatever *other* structures, less capable of exposition, must (we may suppose) simultaneously belong to and operate in the poem.

It is arguable that in recent decades there has been considerable improvement in techniques and devices for the exposition of poetic structure and that many further developments are to be expected. But an account of a poem's structure, however refined and exact it may appear, has still only a limited claim upon the readers to whom it is offered. We may well ponder Poe's phrase "attained its ultimate point of completion." When is a poem finished? When is any interpretation of it complete? "As far as it can go"—is that the same as "on arrival"? Charles Sanders Pierce's doctrine of the extendible interpretant* is highly relevant here.

Moreover, the most discussed poet of my time, in his Minnesota lecture, has justly and refreshingly remarked: "I suspect, in fact, that a good deal of the value of an interpretation is—that it should be my own interpretation." † Whatever accounts are offered to the reader must leave him—in a very deep sense —free to choose, though they may supply wherewithal for exercise of choice.

* "Any given sign admits of *alternative* interpretations; it can be developed, in combination with different groups of further signs, in many different ways . . . in general every sign is a phase in a conversation to which there can be no necessarily last term." W. B. Gallie, *Pierce and Pragmatism,* pp. 124–7.

† T. S. Eliot, *On Poetry and Poets,* p. 114.

This is not—dare I note?—any general license to readers to differ as they please or in other ways and over other points than they must. For this deep freedom in reading is made possible only by the widest surface conformities: as to how the words in a poem are recognised, as to how surface (plain sense) meanings are ascribed, as to how rhythms are followed, allusions caught, cognates given their weight, metaphors taken in, rhetorical parallelisms and oppositions obeyed and so forth, throughout all the machinations. The "wheels and pinions" must be allowed to operate. A whimsical reader may wish, if he likes, that Blake had written:

> Can I see a falling bear
> And not feel my sorrow's share?

But Blake wrote *tear* not *bear*. For all our freedom we are trying to read "the same poem"—mysterious though these words 'the same poem' will ever be. When a reader understands, *e.g.,*

> Pipit sate upright in her chair

in a fashion which connects *sate* with *satiation,* we are, I think, entitled to decide that he is not reading the same poem we are.

In the hope that they may help in exploring the question "What may and what may not be in a poem?" I am adding sundry glosses and commentaries as Notes. I do not feel that this is any disguise either for my expository manoeuvres or for the poems they are concerned with. Needless to say, explanations will never *prove* any poem to be better (or worse either) than it would have been without them. Explanations may make them *seem* more interesting, or less, but that is another matter. Explanations can do little more than play with surfaces. But it is through surfaces (is it not?) that we have to attempt to go deeper. An interest in justness of reading should not neglect the peculiar sources of information under the poet's sole control. Disclaimers of such information have sometimes been fashionable, but they have not as a rule been highly convincing. The poet may, let us grant, be mistaken in what he may later think about meanings in his work. But it would be strange if he often were. More likely, he despairs of reporting the complexity of the considerations which were at work and falls back upon what he hopes are harmless and acceptable simplifications. Coleridge's scandalous remark is in point here: "Poetry gives most pleasure when only generally and not perfectly understood." Faint stars are seen best when you do not stare at them too directly. These doubts spring from a fear. I have met of late too many who start analysing a poem before they have read it. The hustle of an examination room seems not far enough away.

With these and some even less manageable considerations in mind I put these compositions and my Notes before the reader. He may perhaps overhear a continuing internal dialogue directing the order the pieces follow. They attempt to reinforce and to correct one another. I am indebted to the editors of *The New Statesman, Encounter, The Listener, The Yale Review,* and *Audience,* in which some of them have separately appeared. "Only generally and not perfectly understood": I hear the warning. What a strange dream that ! perfectly understood ! evokes. Who dare imagine such understanding? I take comfort from the old Scots proverb "Ilka man buckles his belt his ain gate."

I.A.R.

Arolla, Switzerland
August 10, 1958

Tread out a marble hollow
   Then lay the twigs athwart,
      Teepee-wise or wigwam,
So that the air can follow
   The match-flame from the start:
      As we begin a poem
   And some may win a heart.

For twig to twig will beckon
   If lightly laid above
Better than you can reckon.
      Waste no time devising.
   No, no, it is not love,
      But the drying fume arising
   If the draft be free enough.

As the under cavern reddens
   Leave well alone!
Cold fuel only deadens.
      But pile across the smoke
   And give the dog a bone.
      For its life's sake, don't poke!
The wise fire knows its own.

The wise poem knows its father
   And treats him not amiss;
      But Language is its mother
To burn where it would rather
   Choose that and by-pass this
      Only afraid of smother
Though the thickening snow-flakes hiss.

From committee-doodled day
Beckon'd by the cocktail roar,
Feeling for what seemed a way,
I groped, as I had groped before.
A vivid Presence in the grass
Held me up. I could not pass.

A solitary Daffodil!
Its candid countenance was there
Speaking of the end of ill
With mild, confiding, tranquil air:
Its crisp, translucent whorls so pure
I grew as sure as it was sure.

Through golden depths *on on* it spoke,
A little Trumpet, grave and deep,
And nodded lightly as it woke
The world from transcendental sleep.
Alone had it been waiting there
A Herald and a Harbinger.

So, as a lost word found can say
The never-so-well-known-before,
It welcomed me into a Day
And almost opened me a Door
Through which I may still step to be
In recollected Company.

On the packed trod, the fern
- Beside the crushing boot -
Its should-be crosier'd frond will turn. . .
Turn as a serpent's coil
And grope down through the soil
To re-embrace its root
Renounce the light and air
And its own self inter.
A self itself inter!

Regard this seedling oak.
Busy improvident sheep
The should-be guardian netting broke
Young hopeful twigs to lop
And scalloped leafits crop.
What in the limbs' wide sweep
And oakly dignity,
Stems from such infancy
Grows from calamity?

In the cavern gulfs of thought
- Whatever stir unheard -
The should-be sunlike luminary sought
Flits off as spark from flint
Or the billion-year-old glint
From an inapprehensible Word;
Though new as our morning sky
To some Martian saucering nigh
Meseem as I saunter by.

Years gone, this Spring in me
Dared hardly greet the May
May's should-be summoning breath would flee

Like an unwanted wish
Fishing for so long a fish
It warned all wishes away.
Come Spring, sing clear of Winter
And your own self enter.
Spring into Spring enter!

FORFEITS

Here is a thing;
And a very pretty thing;
What shall I do with
This very pretty thing?

What have I in my hand?
Staff of command?
Ho! Ho! Field Marshal, let,
Let call
This collieshangie off
Before worse harm.
Let beat retreat.
To dodge defeat,
Today,
The only way
Is only to Disarm!

Here is a thing;
And a very pretty thing;
What shall I do with
This very pretty thing?

What have I in my hand?
A baton to conduct
What I select?
Ha! Kappelmeister, set
Our wishes in array,
Duly in line,
And then let
Them
Intone
Their own
Fine
Requiem!

Here is a thing;
And a very pretty thing;
What shall I do with
This very pretty thing?

Still in my hand!
How lay
This ghost,
Or charm, or sign!
A pretty thing
To cling:
This role, this post
Unknown, unconned.
Lay down, lay down,
Old Clown,
Lay down
That Conjuror's wand!

North Conway Nov. 17, 1957

The poem expands as did the philosophy which failed to instruct Alexander. It quotes Werner Jaeger, The Gospel and Marx, looks to the satisfaction of all desires which know what they want and returns to the night waiting for a dawn which continues the unending cycle.

A stirring year, a brooding year; and what's to be the name?
The son of hope and fear and daring came.
    Cry woe, o would. . .o why?

Designed the Soul and built the Word, invented *have* and *can*
Laying out City and Self on the one enfolding plan:
"The great invention of the Greek was Man."
    Cry woe, o would. . .o why?

To him that hath must be given; but what must be taken away?
And how can power serve those who will only pray?
"To each according to his need . . ." were you due to say?
    Cry woe, o would. . .o why?

May peace and plenty and order and health and justice unending
Truth like the stream laid on, knowledge for ever expanding
Limitless shelves brimming with understanding
    Cry woe, o would. . .o why?

At the fullness of Time (*Cross fingers? Cross thumbs at the
    door*)
The Self itself exhaust. No more. Or
Restore the original thirst, open the void at the core.

O is for open. What's open for this thirst?
What come closer than the best and the worst?
Were these two not co-mingled from the first?
    Cross fingers? Cross thumbs at the door.

The good luck fountain in the glassy sea
Faith posturing to incredulity
Little Jack Horner in the Sacristy
    Cross fingers? Cross thumbs at the door.

Not forget: rack and faggot stem from the cell
And highest he who unattaining fell;
Heaven's figments are ground out in Hell.
    Cross fingers? Cross thumbs at the door.

On, on out to the pre-dawn and the reborn air
Where Spring (*O would. . .*) comes to the heart grown bare
Wakes it, washes it, makes it ready if it dare.
    Cross fingers and thumbs at the door.

Full again, though, of. . .we may not know what,
Our lot: we drank too deep of Lethe and forgot.

Legs be still!
Far enough you've walked
Under, up and across
Hill over hill.

What! Are you twitching still?

Heart be still!
Times enough you have balked
Battened on mortal dross
Gobbled your fill.

What! Are you hungry still?

Tongue be still!
Long enough have you talked
Laying out gain and loss
Wish beside will. . .

Would you prophesy still?

Mind be still!

*Aristotle and the Buddha, though poles apart, recom-
mended something describable as the Middle Way:
but did not themselves pursue it. Yet without such,
how could we balance our self-esteem with our hu-
mility?*

Still Golden is the Mean
  Golden the Mean,
Noble the *Eight Fold Path,* the *Middle Way*
  Across the earthly Scene,
These eddying Depths between;
    Though They
  The *Master* and the *Lord*
Who taught men so found each a different ford.

The Master of those who know
  (Defining thus *to know*)
Set up his Self-Regarding Orb for us to gaze at
  Desiring which we grow
  More like it. Even so.
    Was that
  The *Practice of the Mean?*
Conduct for men who should not overween?

And He the *Awakened One.*
  Forsaking Wife and Son
Risked All upon his own unholpen Will
  To kill each spark (or Sun)
  Whereby men seek or shun
    Until
  The very *Seed of Sorrow*
Desire itself, cut off its own to-morrow.

Can men like these be seen
   Stepping a Mean?
Were they not Gods, godless as Gods, again?
   Setting aside the *Screen*
   Re-entering the *Serene?*
      Yet when
Were any who essayed
What such exorbitance would win betrayed?

   Still depths askantly eyed
   Our prudent steps beside -
Staying the promise of Hope with the threat of Fear -
   Assign poor human Pride
   Its Scale thus rectified
      To Hear:
All *Comprehension* is to our wise *Guess*
As that in turn to random *Senselessness.*

"That Other Shore, or Farther Bank, is the realm of ulti-
mate truth and transcendental reality in contradistinction
to This Shore—the bank on which we are standing, mov-
ing and talking, fettered by desire, subject to suffering."—
Heinrich Zimmer: *Myths and Symbols in Indian Art and
Civilization.*

"Here or Nowhere is America."—Goethe.

Those Masters of that Farther Shore
Timeless at length
Forget all time
And all o'ercome before:
Lost is the Life and lost the Loss
And the journey across.

Benign, insuperable, Sublime,
They have the Strength
In Life to kill it
While up its dying boughs they climb.
Yet when they're there they know
It was none of it so.

No Life, no struggle to unwill it,
No length or Strength,
No voyage and no Shore,
No yonder
And no here,

No less, no more
No Law, no errors to fulfil it,
No Climb, no World, no World-forsaking
And no Awakening.
All Worth
Dissolved in Mirth -
All they knew, with all that knew, is gone,
The Scene, the Stage, such things might linger on.

THE THRONE

Not Eve herself is more
Than these Far-Shoremen are
The placard of a Dream
Set up this side the Stream
- Here, on this Hither Shore -
Man's hopes and aims to bar
And scenery to mar.

Nor is it less Desire
- The burning hand and eye -
Designs these Posters here
In outcries of despair:
"Put out, put out the Fire!"
Our Selves to twist awry
And Destiny deny.

The Tongue - itself a flame
And hotter when it's still -
Heats the insurgent Heart
- Silent on either part -
Until white-lit to claim
Through the usurping Will
Old shoes we cannot fill.

Not so the Lotus Throne
Or Who dream-wakes thereon
See now between the Two
- Look we both at and through
Bronze or lacquer or stone -
Within the hither and yon
Seeker become the Known.

O tongue-tip hung the word sublime
　　Would sum-up all All would have said
While temples tumbled on through time
　　And tombs were buried with their dead.

Chance shakes none that; but - know no doubt -
　　Design alone will not avail.
Though their each move be worked right out
　　The servants of my servants fail;

And they I am. What we have been
　　Stands here to limit what we tell
Unless, unless . . . that random scene
　　Re-utter us and all be well.

GOODBYE EARTH:
FAREWELL TO THE PLANET

HAMLET: . . . we defy augury; there's a special providence in the fall of a sparrow. If it be now, 'tis not to come; if it be not to come, it will be now; if it be not now, yet it will come: the readiness is all. Since no man has aught of what he leaves, what is't to leave betimes? Let be.

My space-ship waits, as it has waited long
- Long by the shrinking measure of my days -
Gone like an hour with this much shift of focus:
(By such co-shift Nature her Rule obeys.
By such, my ship, against all strain be strong.)

Gone, as an hour resounding with these quarters:
PRAISE - BLAME: twenty years to which I still belong;
PRAISE - BLAME, TRUE - FALSE: tracking the branching hope;
PRAISE - BLAME, TRUE - FALSE, FAIR - FOUL: wider the scope;
Soon now: PRAISE - BLAME, TRUE - FALSE, FAIR - FOUL,
   RIGHT - WRONG.

My hour speeds; but what O'clock it is,
To whoso could tell Time, I wouldn't know,
Being content the load's that much the lighter.
Space-ships are like a climber's sack in this:
Weight times lift times drop is how you go.

Here's the short list of what's to come - and *there*
The unlistable limitless pile to be left behind.
Don't press too hard to be told exactly why
Which things are still with which. You don't ask: "Where?"
Wantonly, in chat with the newly blind.

On the short list all is nameless. Write it out
And it's all sigils, each of which will mean
Whatever it wants to and the rest will let it.
The unlistable's all nameable - swings between
The unnamed and the named - is not in doubt.

93

What goes with me's myself and that alone:
Something to which it has not set a bound;
Though yet (Hurrah? Alack?) escapable.
It has been lost. It can be, must be found:
This path between a nescience and the known.

The pathless wild the *distant* heart rejoices;
Step in it and there's nothing like a trail.
Earth's finest paths are footworn. This is footless;
Though travelled till it's smoother than a rail:
The outcome of a billion wayward choices.

These choices, made here on our earth, choose still
The circuits out of which my space-ship's built.
Those engineers tried hard to make it simple;
But - Choice of Choices! Milky Way be Spilt! -
Nothing's more complex than the conscious Will:

Exonerate, exempt, self-selfed, self-slain;
The mutinous snow-flake bent upon a mission:
To run a cell, then crawl, a Hamlet, soon
- Its aptitudes all products of division -
Now new designed to be project again.

"But flesh and blood won't whizz off to the stars!"
"Why should they if a figure be the key?
For same is same, alike both here and there."
Yet though that scrap of logic set us free
Nothing can prove that nothing else debars.

Though astronomic statisticians tell us
A million million planets offer life
The raw materials out of which life builds
The home, the battle field, the tissued strife,
The symbiotic tensions that impel us,

New worlds are but the latest, least, excuses
My space-boat does not need. Better far -
Here let me shadow inward in their order,
Since these its cargo and its members are
(From now on anchorless) - the older uses:

SUCCESS, ADVENTURE, FAILURE, COMPREHENDING.
Early SUCCESS, since nothing disillusions
Like getting what you thought it was you wanted,
While you the you are still of your confusions:
The Troilus of the act before the ending.

ADVENTURE then - since loss like this still brings
The chancy source for what men may begin
To audit by a more august ambition.
Near-sighted views of power were old sin
And Shakespeare's mightiest puppets are but Kings.

FAILURE foreseen, forefelt (forfeit forepaid):
There are responsibilities that are not ours
Whate'er our share; though our devout desires
Have their authority, though faint our powers,
Though woe worse woe were were they not gainsaid.

This COMPREHENDING knows not what it knows
Nor what its knowing is - and knows thereby:
Knows ultimately as a planet spins
Or virus thrives; knows how to shut down "Why?"
And mind its crescent business to the close.

There was a time (No, not when Wordsworth sported
And played what games upon that Ocean's shore
- That Ocean my space-ship has yet to traverse -
But well within my Hour) when before
The growing-up of Man men stood transported.

Man grows up fast but men, alas, do not
(Or all too few to make that difference;
A saint, a scientist or two may daunt us).
Meanwhile mankind persists on sufferance
And takes its chance and the stake's all the lot.

Yet Man's a god - tho' men be pismires yet -
A perishable god whose clumsy hand
Could remake anything or ruin it,
Himself above all else. How understand
How so much can in such a grasp be set?

How, silently, in the framing of a verse,
The ordering of a meal, the choice
Of this street or another for a stroll,
In the relaxing moment, speaks the voice
To save or doom - and would we not rehearse?

'If . . . but' well balances 'But . . . if'
                                    Ha! VAULT
OF HEAVEN! GRAND BUBBLE-SHELL EXPAND!
The journey's started
                and what's
                        left's
                            undone.
One's own undoing one could understand.
Leaf falling to the compost finds no fault:

Though not to've known even of what befell!
Flung out beyond the carry of any cry,
Soundless, lightless . . . lifeless - but to try
To win the Mercy in the wish, Goodbye,
And blessing welling from the word, Farewell.

NOT NO

*The mind is compared to a deserted house animated
by the piping of the gales. Responses to this view and
to replies to them and to whatever may utter itself in
this image are included.*

Hail winds, who've found your keyhole and your key!
Found out! - Through what forgotten clue it show -
Through *x* without or *y* within to know:
Not mine this life that must be lived in me.

Inside as out Another's: let it be.
Ha, Skater on the Brink!
                              Come whence,
                                        Where go?

Anywhere
            Elsewhere
                        Where I would not know
Not mine, not mine, all this lived through in me.

Who asks? Who answers? What ventriloquy!
Not that, not that - that's only undertow
Though through such duct must you or I outflow
(Unheard! Unknown!) who live through this in me.

No argument for immortality
In what you owe who might through these words see?

RETORT

"Eternity is in love with the productions of Time."
—*Proverb of Hell.*

A poem's not on a page
    Or in a reader's eye;
   Nor in a poet's mind
Its freedom may engage.
    For I, a poem, I
   Myself alone can find
   Myself alone could bind.

I, though I take from you
    All, all I have to sing,
   Am all an empty Ought
Spinning itself its clew.
    Burning up what you bring
   To search out what you sought,
   I work on out from naught.

Eyeless, a source of seeing,
    Careless, a fount of care,
   An unrecorded vow
Is all my core of being.
    Yet, neither here nor there
   And with no then but now,
   Your life I disallow.

I sing, who nevertheless
    No accents have or breath.
   I neither live nor die.
But you whom I possess. . .
    You, you know life and death
   And throughly know; so I
   What void I fill thereby.

Ah yes, the heart-ache friend
  Out there before you:
    The light-handed
      World-worn
    Nimble-witted
      Thrice-born
Comprehending, leisurable mind;
All yours and
  Eager to adore you.

Turn up the light!
O it is you there
You again
To whom each care:
  The dodging hope
The thin insight
  The narrowed scope
The famished wish
  The maiming shame
The bare despair,
  So freely came.

Who is the third
Stands by without a word?
Who watches this mistake?

How see the familiar I
Peer almost hourly through itself
Then sigh
Then steal and steel its own one eye:

In this world wake
In that world sleep
Each pervious to the other's ache.
- Who weaves this spell? -
How see all this and yet not see as well!

December–April 1953–4

Still missing it though:
Though what, none know.
Still journeying on:
On what commission?
Still hoping to be There
Ere we Be anywhere;
And waiting till an Hour
Our idleness empower:
For Place and Hour and We
We seek at best to be
Being a-want, all three
And indiscernably.

Home again?
How?
How timorously
My wishes climb
The overhanging *if*
Or *when;*
How perilously.

So. Let them be.
Let me not be
A while-keeper
Who keeps accounts with time.

Come again?
Gone!
On, anywhere -
As if hard-pressed,
As if in debt, in love
With *then,*
In fear of *here;*
Though everywhere
Is here, when there;
And presently
This "this" is all the rest.

Savings none?
None
Accountable.
Past hunger's past.
The left, the lost
(Amen)
Irrecoverable

Renounced as well;
The possible
Our modicum
For this spent life at last.

I

The unmentionable is with, in, of me: me.
The mentionable turns object, over against;
Not me, not me: my shell.
And we who mention, we,
Are never what is mentioned.
What pure eye
Ever yet beheld the beholder?

My woven and compacted shell,
My global roof,
I tap and probe.
My diamond drill
Billions of light years off
Brings in its proof.
Uncrackable
And well
Defended still,
It is
This shell.

How not behold the beholder?
My extant shell
That Eye projects;
Its diamond rays
Billions of lifetimes older
That shell reflects.
What's kept, it says,
By what is scrapped,
It says,
Is kept.

Hill, cloud, field, wall. . .
All that we touch, see, think. . .
Unliven all: the stone, the dust
The Earth itself and men and Man
Turn thing
And must.

Will, doubt, desire, thought. . .
All in us:
Faith, Hope, Love. . .
Naught but THINGS itself away
And you, and I, as meant, obey:
Are noun'd
To naught.

Meanwhile,
Hill, cloud, field, wall. . .
As word with word
Unmeant, unheard, unseen,
Will, willy-nilly, mean.

*King Acrisius, being warned that he would die by the
hand of his daughter's son, imprisoned Danae in a
Tower of Brass inaccessible to all men. But Zeus
visited her; and Perseus, who was set adrift on the sea
at his birth, and preserved through many adventures,
came at last unknown before King Acrisius at Argos.
There in the games, his cast so far outflew all others
that the discus fell on the King's instep and killed him.*

Walled up, walled in, the maiden doom
   The King, her father, dares not kill;
   Ruefully subject to his will,
Secure, he thinks, as his own tomb.

But, but within all let or lour,
   There rules an order without bound:
   Cyclic, unsearchable, but found
When the unthinkable junctures flower.

And startling as the fore-felt rime
   The sense resists and would refuse
   Justly and when it's due to lose
The step denied steps in in time.

Welcome as wind-borne pollen shower
   The Cloud-bringer - O clouds unfurl! -
   Comes in upon the waiting girl
And puts to shame that Brazen Tower.

The Golden Shower; the Virgin Birth;
   The Infant Voyage: what Moses in you all
   But draws his power thence? his Call
Clearer; firmer his title to the Earth.

Acrisius you! That daughter thought
  The King in you would still confine
  In loth foreknowledge from her line
Will come your deathblow - as it ought.

Be welcome, unknown shoot of ours,
  Before our footstool when you stand.
  Here is the discus to your hand:
To the casting line! Run out the hours!

Athens, July 2—Pontresina,
Samedan, July 14 '55

107

It creaked all night with cautious steps,
    The house, my mind, the world without,
Where all stood still the years I slept
    Dreamless, in triple doubt of doubt,

Waiting to wake. Awake to wait,
    Set to listen though not warned why,
Tiptoeing on in the Blind Man's maze. . .
    What breathed as I tiptoed by?

Whirl! Whatever it was was scared!
    Whirl'd as I in the self-same spin!
Or hearkens my heart-thumps where I stare,
    Quivers within my bristling skin,

Where I - house, world, all, in hand -
    Trigger'd to wipe out Now and Here,
Listening-post to my own command,
    Stand by, cramped in the fear of fear.

Harvard. January, 1958.

> Let it work;
> For 'tis the sport to have the enginer
> Hoist with his own petar. And't shall go hard
> But I will delve one yard below their mines
> And blow them at the moon.

> *—Hamlet, III, iv, 205–8*

Pristine. . .benign,
As ever, dawn;
And this last eve
That's. . .not an eve.

After no little
Reprieve,
Nothing to follow;
Nothing to flow:
Suddenly solid.
Solid and brittle.

Lucid and still,
No more at stake.

Time to await,
Tranquil, if chill,
What cannot be late.

Doubtless as spectacle
Beyond ad. supreme,
Wholly lost word,
Out of that world.

Out with it too
So in the dream
So did we will,
Firmly astute,
Taking the long view.

109

Twenty second minute
From the petar's pad. . .

Now. . .how. . .awake.

OUTCAST

And they set the ark of God on a new cart and brought it out of the house of Abinadab. . . . And David and all the house of Israel played before the LORD. . . . And when they came to Nachon's threshing floor, Uzzah put forth his hand to the ark . . . for the oxen shook it. . . . And the anger of the LORD was kindled against Uzzah and God smote him there for his error; and there he died by the ark of God.—*II Samuel* 6:3–7.

Outside the Wall
Insuperable,
Before the Gate
The trio stood;
Their fate
To band too late
To plot -
Not as they would
But as they might:

Each hand
Against each hand
Again.

They stood
They stand:
Bare Myth
Sheer Creed
Mere Rite:

Where we
(Who are they)
May underhear,
Nay, be
Their Colloquy.

While I (who am Myth) await
A myth to tell our fate,

And I (who am Creed) reveal
Old wounds we cannot heal,
I (who am Rite) enact
Our inoperable pact.
So we who could profess
Now but co-confess.

O Rite and Myth and Creed
Comfort you one another
Comfort you in your need
And one another lead.
O Myth and Creed and Rite
Sightless the sightless lending light
O Creed and Rite and Myth
Nearer than Kin or Kith

Salute, receive, believe. . .

The Wall, the Leaden Gate
The City State:

Within,
Where none may live,
Thought engines spin and weave.

Within their compassing
What is there you could bring?

Keeping their mathematics warm
Within the magnetic sieve
The ultimate plasma-swarm.

> Poor Uzzah's ark
> Reborn
> This myth
> - But with
> More mortal spark
> Forlorn.

Balanced up somehow on a ball
  That spins
    And spirals
      As it plummets,
  Newton walked to Stourbridge Fair
  And bought his prism
That was to fell the founding wall
  Undo the
    All
  Renew the
    Fall
      Bound through all limits
  And far and here declare
    The mere abysm.

Without——within! We were that idle void
  Its dust
    Its ashes
      Its endurances
  Its fled shrunk coils of stars
    Its wistlessness
Till we our Selves destroyed.
  The net
    We knit
  To sweep
    The deep
      Outwit the yet-perchances
  Took with it what else bars
    Existlessness.

O sole observer! Only unobserved!
  Neglected
    Left out
      Son of trouble!

113

O knower glassier than the wave
  You float on,
Fish-serpent, winged and nerved,
  Invisible
    But still
  The source (which way
    you will)
      Of each least pressure building in the bubble:
  Is it not time to try your brave
    New coat on?

Open, entire, surrendered and serene
  "Seemeth"
    And maybe
      "That concordant one,"
  Unlatched, a-swing to whatso'er
    Might lurk without.
But what's left out when naught's within?
  The sky
    Washed clean
  The dry
    Staff green,
      The circle won,
The pure light blossoms everywhere
  Out of the doubt.

Up through the gulf of air
The torrents' roar
Draws near
Or
Fades away
As the winds veer.

Time's rising gale
Has hold. Peak following peak:
Bleak sail outspread:
Cold walls await
A sunrise always late;
Then take in turn the red,
The gold, the bright
Insufferable light;
Turn on through noon,
Through afternoon;
With stretching shade
Engage
The edge of night,
Regain
The red,
The stain
Soon
Dead,
Maintain
Their Kinship with the Moon.

Up near the ridges
Ruin's on display
In toppling block
And rockfall smoking down to join the scree;
But hides his sway,

More murderous in the hay.
Time's scythings must engrave
The clean uncrumpled slopes;
Each swash or swathe
Ravage must be
To howsomany thriving creature's hopes
And an old 'out' for those who could not thrive.

Height's on display as well;
And depth,
Clouded or clear,
But sheer:
The full forefigurement of hope and fear.

So Heaven creates its Hell
And Hell its other heaven:
Flat as a penny
Even as Eden
Open to any.

And they who would excel
Whose aspiration was inevitable
Their other tale could tell.

Swift flows the race,
Old Overshot wheels glittering o'er;
With no ill grace
The log draws through the saw.

PERPETUITY

Moment not of being
Out of another time
Under a different sky.

Near-by others floating
Foam astray as I am
Rapt in a bubble of joy,
Of woe, or fear of touching:
Bubbles each other lime
Join and themselves destroy.

Ever and never the same
Water and film and air
Traveller, journey and flow
   (The watcher on the bank
   The hoper and his plank)
Breather and blood and flame
Ash into flight into fire
Reaping to plough and to sow.
Name, go dance with name!
Plenty weeps with desire
Ago and again ago.

In perpetuity
Be here their prayer:
   May *may* become
   While *would* would waft
   Or let *let* be
Our sum   our raft   our quay.

About the boundless yard may trudge
But victim, culprit, hangman, judge.

Victim rejoice! Your bitter end
Helps the primal hurt mend.

And culprit sing: "Traitor's blow
Cuts through knots in Even So."

Grave hangman smile: your gentle hands
Loose the noose none withstands.

But of the Judge, whom all must seek,
Little of him do wise men speak.

Victim and culprit, hangman too,
All in one, here go you.

About the groundlessness go spin,
Who bear no grudge and hear no sin.
Become the Self itself shall judge.

THE RUINS

The taste of time's beyond our wit
Like the lamb's bleat, the donkey's bray
A-sway on the edge of the eternal wall
Soon earthquake-juggled crazy; like the stray
Verse that if it could would say it.

The broken nose and the lost hand
May now enhance the statue's pose:
See for yourselves you may and take
Your own good will for deed - by those
Connivances our weakness won't withstand.

Nor scorn the syllables defective here
To take a sly advantage of their fault:
Blackleg a local strike or so, they will,
Or jerry-rig; since to the dear deaf ear
All words come cuckooing out of the same vault.

You do not trade too long upon a lack,
And words in poems have rights, say out their say,
Exact and render strict account,
Have little mercy on what's seen its day
Or could betray: all in the troth of the pack.

Sometimes a word is wiser much than men:
"Faithful" e.g., "responsible" and "true."
And words it is, not poets, make up poems.
Our words, we say, but we are theirs too
For words made man and may unmake again.

To be at once explicit and elliptic
Both they and we play spillikins today
In homage to the log-jam and the landslide:

119

Lost nestless ants aclambering in the hay
Where some old, rusty, parting wire has flipt it.

So which way's which is now no more a query
And up or down's as free as heads or tails.
Without a center or a pull to check it
The very sense of that dimension fails:
Rise! Fall! Sink - swim? All idle theory.

To take its place we have a wide selection
Of sweepings from the folklore merchants' floors
Pickings from anthropology's kitchen midden.
Come, cross yourselves at the museum doors
Before you add yourselves to the collection!

Did science answer only as to science
A faith could keep its converse for its own.
But "WHAT AM I?" is the end of all enquiry
And what it turns on straight is turned to stone.
(A Gorgon of that grade's no mean appliance).

Ah! deadliest aid to mental indigestion,
Solvent can settle all, beside yourself -
Nothing whatever left upon the tapis,
Were you not firmly kept upon the shelf:
What's made you ask yourself your final question?

In the museum now. And no one's here
Who isn't in for life - as an exhibit,
As a museum, no less, without the labels.
Museum specimens! Should the thought inhibit?
What has an instance left to hope or fear?

Round us in the clear and lighted spaces
The bones of statuary appear to stand
Stripped clean of the original blaze of colour
And dressed anew by Time's irreverent hand
To match the hid amazement on their faces:

120

"Never to be more honored or regaled!
For all we were to have no mediation!
No solace but your impotent regard!
Poor token of your blinded adoration
Had you beheld before our beauty failed!

"The ecstasies our sanctuaries cherished
Were not as yours (for you have yours, no doubt
Beyond the compass of our divination)
What makes you go about so and about
To care so much for so much that has perished?"

Now their high structures all asprawl lie scattered,
Palace and temple, débris in the sun;
The faiths they sheltered every bit as weathered,
Disjointed just as much by excavation:
As if the record were the thing that mattered.

We excavators are in ruins too
Would need some rare successor to restore us
- Suppose he found our remnants worth his trouble -
"Judge not and ye shall not be judged." It's true;
On each research research in turn is due.

Leave us well hid beneath our heaps of rubble.

Odysseus chose the lot that's out of view:
Happy the town or man sans history.
Maybe none's such and the least thing we do
Or leave undone within this mystery,
So burry is the seed, is sifted through.
So leads this parable - by the fall-line too:
"All's all rehearsal for the grand adieu."

June '55: Delphi, Parnassus, Knossos, Epidaurus, Cyllene

Welcome the Fool's own Cap,
The stuffed and prick't-up Ear,
All-hail each hissing Bell,
Caper and Crow and Leer!
From now on, what I mean to mean,
From now on, none can tell,
   No one can tell.

Bless those Behaviorists
Who made us out all *Jack*
(*a-Lantern & o'clock*)
Our only Wear, Good-lack!
- Benefit of Clergy now being out -
To save us in the Dock.

Here's to old Flesh and Blood
That do so deep deceive
Heaven and Earth and Hell!
Beauty's Eyes you do believe
Though what their Tears or Smiles can prove
Why none, no, none can tell,
   No one can tell.

Cunninger still the Verse
When with its ruddering Rime
From perjured Breath it wrings
Sincerity sublime.
You'ld think a Poet had an End
In View in what he sings.

So then, in what I write,
Look! Look not for me.
My Lines will do as well,
Let them as well go free;
They say whatever they chance to say
And what more none can tell,
    No, none can tell.

What none will say
        Except in verse
                Terse and succinct:
                "How gay this wraith,
Going away
        From scene to place
                        Grace be, unlink't!"
                In his each breath

What's past its use
        Let out must be,
                Free, since refùsed:
                Réfuse at play.
Why should he choose
        Not to be gone
                        On - being used
                To the get-away?

Used too to rumour
        Echo reverse
                Rehearsal alert
                To the camp of breath.
Decamp in time
        Who unconcerned
                Have learned from birth
To find your rime.

HARVARD YARD IN APRIL:
APRIL IN HARVARD YARD

To and fro
Across the fretted snow
Figures, footprints, shadows go.

Their python boughs a-sway
The fountain elms cascade
In swinging lattices of shade
Where this or that or the other thought
Might perch and rest.
                And rest they ought
For poise or reach.
Not all is timely. See, the beech,
In frosty elephantine skin
Still winter-sealed, will not begin
Though silt the alleys hour on hour
Débris of the fallen flower,
And other flowery allure
Lounge sunlit on the Steps and there
Degrees of loneliness confer.

Lest, lest. . .away!
You may
Be lost by May.

Brimful of abandoned hope
These silver trees will sail
Their sudden crowding fleet aloft:
Then gaily on the gale
They'll spill the wreckage down the slope.

Heartfelt our faltering glance
Catches the flash and fall.
No Will-you—Won't-you paltering there!
"All *out,* no *in!*" The call
Could tempt a heart to join that dance.

No, no, old snowflake thought!
Whatever you still must do,
Or say, or be, has still its right.
That flaunt is not for you,
Who, in an ampler gamble caught,
Live with a doubtfuller end in sight.

FALL SONG

Breathing in and out
Morning, noon and night.
Coming, now, and gone:
Springtide, Summer, Fall.
Promise, power, praise;
Subject, verb, and close.

Who knew all three
He only
Could justly speak for all
And tell
Some truth about the Fall
And what it was befell.

Fat kine, then lean;
In token?
And that grey age an ash?
Or crown?
And those young fires, desires
For dutiful years to drown?

Looked forward to,
Tomorrow
Came not as you had seen;
Long feared,
The ultimate chagrin
Grew other as it neared.

Slow come; quick gone!
Anon
A sunset flush will stain
The slide.
What you would ascertain
Time's conjuring would hide.

Forget, forget. . . Forget what you forget.
The diary entry: name, fact, place and date
Let go and let the loitering dead be dead.

Missed cue, lost quote, worst muddled figures yet,
The choice statistic, much mislaid of late,
Forget, forget. . . Forget what you forget.

The side-long glance, the sigh, the oblique head,
The lifeless tone you could anticipate
Let go and let the loitering dead be dead.

The hidden face, the word too gently said
That spelled maybe a formula of fate
Forget, forget. . . Forget what you forget.

Why should they haunt you, hold you in their debt,
Remind you of their loss?   The debt is paid.
Let go and let the loitering dead be dead.

All feeling now like foliage to be shed.
Did you forget regret as well must fade?
Let go and let the loitering dead be dead.
Forget, forget. . . Forget what you forget.

There was a young fellow went by:
Alight his eye
And his step was free.
But what could he see?
What could he be?
Ah, me!

Here's an old buffer drawn near:
Oh, dear,
Do what he will
He sees less still!

In between:
The man,
Firm and cool:
Their measure and their mean:
Green
And a fool.

Any day now
When all is said and done
The three
Will be
One
With Nineveh
And Tyre and Babylon;
As - in a different way,
But who knows how? -
They
Under their
Self-same star
Were
And are.

Farewell, young Muse! you've teased me long enough,
Promising lines and rimes you didn't furnish.
You claimed you had some public's ear as well.
You've pestered me to clip and file and burnish
But rust adorns, I find, and dust's the stuff.

You've lectured me on What and How and Why
Until there's not a theme I care to touch.
Artful and heartless, innocent and sly
Go decorate some other poet's couch
Now all is almost over. Here! Goodbye!

Go wrench his sense and regulate his voice.
Tell him there's nothing left for verse to say
Though only you can find the way to say it.
Give him my greeting with your rates of pay
And never let him know he has no choice.

NOTES

They all muddy the water that it
may seem deep . . .

They have learned from the sea its vanity too:
is not the sea the peacock of peacocks?

Even before the ugliest of all buffaloes
does it spread out its tail: never
does it tire of its lace-fan of silver
and silk.
                    —Zarathustra on Poets

LIGHTING FIRES IN SNOW

This practical poem aims to teach a useful art.

THE SOLITARY DAFFODIL

This visitant appeared in 1957 without precedent in the waste area, once a garden, beside my office. As I was studying it an unknown passer-by remarked: "Writing a poem; you should!" and went on his way. He seemed to me as visionary as the flower. Symmetry with its Companion Piece was part of the design from the first.

whorl: generically, a convolution, coil, curl; especially of something suggesting a turning or whirling movement; here a celestial rather than a botanical description.

And the spindle turns round upon the knees of Necessity. On every one of its circles is a Siren, who travels round with the circle, and cries out on one note, and the eight notes are joined in one harmony. And round about are seated at equal distances the Fates, the daughters of Necessity, Lachesis, Clotho and Atropos; who, clothed in white robes, with flowers on their heads, keep harmony in their song with the music of the Sirens. And the song of Lachesis is of the past; that of Clotho, of the present; that of Atropos, of the future. And Clotho with her right hand helps to turn the outer edge of the whorl, stopping from time to time, and Atropos with her left hand turns the inner circles, while Lachesis in turn helps one or the other.

—Republic, 617.

BRACKENCLOSE

The title is both the name of the Hut built amid a grove of fine oaks above Wastwater by the Fell and Rock Climbing Club of the English Lake District and a reference to the singular conduct of bracken on the footpath.

Much earlier in its life the plant has done something a little like this very successfully:

It is curious to note that the underground habit of the plant does not at once become apparent. It is only after the production of a number of the

133

leaves that the stem divides into two branches which grow downwards into the soil, whence they never again come up into the light.

—S. Leonard Bastin, *Flowerless Plants,* p. 36.

trod: footway or track.

leafits: used of young leaves by Coleridge and Keats; no proposed connection here, in spite of the dictionary, with leaflets as young tracts.

sunlike luminary: the Idea of the Good.

Socrates: Take this as a parallel to the soul. When its attention is on whatever is bright with true being, the soul takes it in, and has deep knowledge of it and seems itself clearly to be full of thought and reason; but when it is turned to the twilight things which come and go, it forms opinions only, its edge is dulled, and first it has one and then another opinion as if it were without thought or reason. This, then, which gives true being to whatever deep knowledge is of, and the power to get this knowledge to whatever gets it, is to be named the Idea of the Good, and you are to see it as being the cause of knowledge, and of what is true in so far as there is knowledge of it. But beautiful though deep knowledge and the true are, you will be right in believing that there is something still more beautiful. And, as it was right before not to take seeing and light to be the sun, though they are sunlike, so here you will take knowledge and the true to be their parallels and like the good, but don't take them to be the good. The good has a still higher place of honor.

Glaucon: Beautiful beyond thought will it have to be, if it is that which gives us knowledge and the true and is still more beautiful than they are. You are certainly not saying that it is pleasure.

Socrates: Hush! But take a look at this parallel farther. The sun, wouldn't you say, not only gives a thing its power to be seen, but its generation and growth, though the sun is not itself generation. So too, you are to say, things are known only because the good is present; both that they are and what they are come from the good. But the good is not being but is far higher in honor and power.

Glaucon: Heavens! That out-tops everything!

Socrates: You forced me to say what my thoughts about it were.

Glaucon: Don't stop. But do at least stretch out the parallel with the sun; if there is anything you are not giving us.

Socrates: Well, in fact, I am letting more than a little go.

—*Republic,* 508–9.

our morning sky: Mars has no atmosphere and a Martian could be surprised by the beauty of Earth's sky.

saunter: origin obscure. 1. To muse, to be in a revery. 2. a. To wander about aimlessly; to travel as a vagrant. b. To walk with a leisurely and careless gait. 3. To loiter over one's work, to dawdle.

134

I like the allegation that it originated in a derisive term for dilatory Crusaders: *Sainte Terre-ers.*

YIN & YANG

The two opposing principles in Chinese culture. Night and day serve as their emblem. Written at Easter in Jerusalem.

he who unattaining fell: Milton's Satan.

too deep:

From there, the souls traveled without turning back under the throne of Necessity. When all had passed, they journeyed into the Levels of Oblivion, through thick, painful heat, for there were no trees or plants; and in the evening they stopped by the River of Unmindfulness whose water no vessel may keep. They were all made to take a measure of the water; those who were not saved by their good sense drank more than the measure, so that all memory of everything went from them.

—*Republic,* 621.

LANDFALL

Compare:

Of that heavenly Wisdom as we then talked and hunger'd after it, lo, with the whole effort of our heart we apprehended somewhat thereof: and we sighed, and abandoning on that far shore those first fruits of the spirit, we fell back to the sound of our own views, and the determinate words of human discourse.

—Augustine, *Confessions,* ix, 10. Robert Bridges' version, *The Spirit of Man,* 32.

GOODBYE EARTH

a million million planets:

Astronomers have reason to believe that a planet such as ours—of about the earth's size and temperature, and about as well lighted—is a rare event in the universe. Indeed, filled as our story is with improbable phenomena, one of the least probable is to have had such a body as the earth to begin with. Yet though this probability is small, the universe is so large that it is conservatively estimated at least 100,000 planets like the earth exist in our galaxy alone. Some 100 million galaxies lie within the range of our most powerful telescopes, so that throughout observable space we can count apparently on the existence of at least 10 million million planets like our own.

—George Wald, "The Origin of Life" in *The Physics and Chemistry of Life,* a Scientific American book, Simon and Schuster. New York, p. 25.

if a figure be the key:

In other words, the fact that we cannot telegraph the pattern of a man from one place to another is probably due to technical difficulties. . . .
—Norbert Wiener, *The Human Use of Human Beings,* p. 110.

what games:

Hence in a season of calm weather
Though inland far we be,
Our Souls have sight of that immortal sea
Which brought us hither,
Can in a moment travel thither,
And see the children sport upon the shore,
And hear the mighty waters rolling evermore.

—*Intimations of Immortality from Recollections of Early Childhood.*

The Troilus of the act before the ending:

Ulysses: All's done, my lord.
Troilus: It is.
Ulysses: Why stay we then?

—*Troilus and Cressida,*
V, ii, 112.

RAINBOW

Lines 5–6 are from an essay by Professor E. G. Boring on the development of psychology.
v. 3, 1.5: I extend the promise made to Noah to include immunity from floods of knowledge about ourselves.
glassier:

Most ignorant of what he's most assured,
His glassy essence

—*Measure for Measure,* II, ii, 120.

v. 4, 11. 2,4: "The Phoenix and the Turtle," line 46.

136

ALPINE SKETCHES

flat as a penny: a sheep farmer from North Wales praised in these words the fenland round Ely.

THE RUINS

the lot that's out of view:

And it chanced that the soul of Odysseus had the last number of all, and came to make its selection. From the memory of the toils of its last life, it had no longer any ambition, and went about everywhere in search of the quiet life of a private person, and was a long time looking till it saw it at last in some out-of-the-way place untouched by the others, and, on seeing it, said that it would have done the same if it had had the first number, and took it gladly.

—Republic, 620.

fall-line: the line by which detached fragments of a mountain will most probably travel.

NONE CAN TELL

Behaviorists: These have, of course, taught that consciousness and all that:

Life, soul, form, spirit, whence they being have;

may as well be regarded as Will-o'-the-Wisp or Jack-o'-Lantern— irrelevant to the proper study of us Jack-o'clocks.

HARVARD YARD IN APRIL: APRIL IN HARVARD YARD

Harvard, the oldest college in the United States (1636) has traditionally maintained the use of the word *Yard.* In establishing Harvard College, the Overseers purchased an "eighth-of-an-acre house-lot and one-acre cowyard behind." This slip of land was promptly christened the College Yard to distinguish it from the cowyards on either side. . . . Around this nucleus the Harvard Yard slowly accrued until, a century ago, it attained the present dimensions. . . . *Yard,* to be sure, was the common English word for an enclosure. . . . There was (and is) a Senate-House Yard at Cambridge, and a College Yard at St. Andrews. But the Harvard Yard was doubtless suggested by . . . cows . . . rather than old-world quads. . . . Other Colonial colleges, too, had their 'yards.' But in 1774, Princeton rejected the homely monosyllable for *campus.* One by one every other American college has followed suit, until Harvard alone has kept her Yard.

—Samuel Eliot Morison, '08, writing in his *Three Centuries of Harvard,* p. 7, and in his *Founding of Harvard College,* pp. 229–230.

The poem began as a *not-at-all* wish-*fulfilling* dream of a spring flight from Harvard—in lines in part retained in the *coda:* something like

> Happiest they
> Who would away
> Who may be gone
> By May

These and similar tentatives were nursed awhile in traverses through the Yard to and from my office—the Yard's character as a pre-eminent locus of *to-and-fro-ing* (physical and spiritual) not coming into clear consciousness until the poem was almost finished. Only then, argument and counter-argument (often not meeting) came to mind as a ground justifying some comparing of the fretted snow with tracked and retracked sheets of paper, together with a feeling that *figures* (line 3) could be numerals. There was earlier an echo from a lecture remark I had made: "The printed words of a poem are only its footprints on paper."

fretted: eat; eat away; consume; torture by gnawing; gnaw at; wear away by friction; chafe; roughen; cause to ripple, as a breeze frets the surface of water; tease; vex; worry . . .

The illuminating Dictionary adds a comment on *gnaw at* which pleased me when I saw it. It says, "Now only of small animals." A mouse, I suppose, can fret a bit of cheese (as a fret saw does plywood); but when a grizzly bear chaws up a man, that isn't fretting. I liked that; it seemed to offer my line a spice of meaning I had not been aware of. It turned the people who had been leaving all those tracks on the snow into only small animals after all and gave a diminishing-glass sharpness to the scene.

Early drafts played with *snakey,* but, with *a-sway, cascade,* and *shade* present, another vowel seemed desirable, and *lithe* and *writhe* (along, perhaps, with *scythe* and *withe*) were active in attempts to describe what was striking me: a movement, at once lively, sinuous and angular. For *snakey,* on the other hand, there was no such morphemic support here; on the contrary: *shakey*—no good at all; *break*—no, no; *fake*—horrors! So *python* boughs it had to be.

a-sway: the slighter motions of bare boughs are more visible before leafage comes, and in spring, when the eye is watching for every advance, there is more occasion than in winter to observe them. Winter gales agitate them, but in spring breezes they seem to stir of their own will with the mounting sap.

cascade: the thickening fringes and tassels of budding leaf and flower on outermost pendent sprays were green or golden drops defining the outline of the fountain's fall; their *shade,* though thin, softening and cooling the glare of sunlight on the snow.

perch: comparison of thoughts with birds seems inevitable. Trumbull Stickney's grand lines, for example:

> Sir, say no more. Within me 'tis as if
> The green and climbing eyesight of a cat
> Crawled near my mind's poor birds.

timely: when thoughts turn to trees, in academic groves at least, Eve and her Tree of Knowledge are not far off. I would like to think that the poem contained originally a suggestion that the Tree (*python boughs*) was itself the Tempter, but that was an afterthought. As yet there is no Fruit (forbidden or not) to these studies, only flower.

silt the alleys: silt proposed itself as suggesting sand—product of breakup, unlubricative, arid, unfruitful; alleys, channels for to-and-fro-ing, worn into grooves, out of true and clogged by the grit of work.

débris: hourly wastage of new, ungerminated, uncared for ideas, which may choke the channels; the wreckage and waste of "essential omission"—to use Whitehead's phrase—the saving neglect, which strains (and trains) the academic.

allure: a lure is an apparatus used to recall hawks, a bunch of feathers within which, during its training, the hawk finds its food. Catachrestically, it can be both a snare and a mark to be shot at. The young scholar might be glad to borrow Cupid's bow to use on selected members of Radcliffe who at this season begin to decorate the Chapel steps in their spring fabrics.

Degrees of loneliness: very different from the degrees that are conferred at Commencement. The line consciously echoed Donne's *The Ecstasy* (line 44) "Defects of loneliness controls."

lost: in terms not only of the allure but of examination results and the perplexities of study.

The Elder Brethren of the Corporation of Trinity House are responsible for lighthouses, pilots and much else that concerns navigation.

THE
SCREENS
AND
OTHER
POEMS

TO
D.E.P.
FARTHER
ALONG
THE
RIDGE

What connections, if any, hold between a critic's theories about poetry and his practice when he professes as a poet? My own view has been that no such connections should be discernible. The duties of good critical theory, I have maintained, are analogous to those of a good police in a society as nearly anarchic as possible. Good theory is not there to tell the poet what he shall do, but to protect him from gangster-theories: academism, punditry, fashion, faction, movements, modernities, and so forth. Critical theory does this best by observing the actualities of inspiration and composition. These, I suggest, are complex enough to make inferences as to how a poet *should* write ridiculous.

The Notes confine themselves to references and lexical indications for readers who may care to use them.

I am indebted to the Editors of *The Atlantic Monthly, The Kenyon Review, Partisan Review,* and *The New Statesman* for permission to include poems which have appeared in their pages.

I. A. R.

BIRTHDAY THOUGHTS

The wind bloweth where it listeth, and thou hearest the
voice thereof, but knowest not whence it cometh, and
whither it goeth: so is every one that is born of the Spirit.
—*John* 3:8

INTRODUCTION

As in some cabinet not far
From his show cases,
The invisible curator places,
Upon its proper shelf
Within its due division, niche or drawer,
Each choice type-specimen Self;

Its ornate, and its not so
Ornate shells,
Its vestures, sociable or else;
Its own interior shield,
Or shields; so well arranged that one might know
All knowable in this field

Merely by due inspection;
But he displays
For public gaze or praise
Only a chosen piece
(Descry who may his process of selection);
I, as no news release,

On this auspicious day
Will here pick out
As more than enough to talk about
But a few themes:
May they, so this exordium would pray,
Be neither schemes nor dreams.

I

Lissom this spring,
Spiral close-curl'd;
Slender: the thing
To hold up a curtain
To shut out a world.

Loop it now. Lay
Coil beside coil:
This day, my birthday,
By those which were theirs,
Those othering "me's"
Of the distancing years.

Nothing more certain
In the mortal turmoil:
No science sees
What can tie
A perennial "I."

Geometrical
Continuity
Can afford the body
A past: we have spun
With our Earth as we
Sped round our Sun.
But, the Identical:
How is that One?

O Nicodemus,
How should these things be?

A coil of coils
Models the track
Of my physical years.
Foil of foils!
For our lack
Nothing appears.

What they missed, those others
    Sharing my birth with me,
Was often enough a gain
    By what I see.

Fortune accorded favors
    In such queer shape:
The triumph, a prison;
    Disaster, escape.

I - to my successor -
    May see all this awry.
Why not? We're not trying
    To see eye to eye.

And what though he forget
    What I care for most
- As I do with theirs,
    Their dread and their boast -

In these diversities
    Lodges our hope:
May even our meanness
    Further the Grope

That fumbles and grasps,
    Takes hold, lets go,
Widelier than any
    One groper can know:

That shifts and returns
    With the veering Earth.
For a Deathday, nightfall;
    For a Birthday, rebirth?

Plato (like Shakespeare)
Rounding up his sphere
Left on the day he came.
Serviceable Fate
To help us celebrate
Made his dates the same.

As serviceably we
May here and now decree
This Janus symbol ours:
Our Entry-Exit Day
From which we would survey
The sources and the prospects of our powers.

But - no repining!
It's but a whining,
Beneath a generous care.
"If only. . . !" - Hush, O hush!
You make the cosmos blush.
No contra-factual implicatives lodge here.

Surely this Day
May beg forbearance
Both of and for
Forbears and descendants.

Summon I dare
Heirs and legators:
Each day - but two - both:
Loth mediators.

Forbear days! You
Through whom I'm here
Handing along our
Powers and our fear,

How may a moment,
In t' motley dressed,
Hint, when forgot,
What might be best?

Predecessors (take heed)
Need no more be dead
Than successors succeed:
Seed ill-sped.

Most children don't now
Bow much to parents.
Most famous men
End up as defendants.

Pledging the future,
Your careless abandon
Squandered the wherewithal
All could now stand on.

Wide off the beam,
Dream confounded,

Seeing no more than I
Why we weren't grounded,

You ruined me
Betimes. Much, much as I,
I, in my turn
Burn what   they'd live by.

Must such be the fashion
(Passion gone sour)
What the movement decrees
Lees of our hour?

Would that all together
Whether this needs be
We might consider
Iteratively!

Since on a Birthday
May a new Day start;
An old lag lapse
Perhaps; *Revenant* depart!

By flooding down my hurry-scurrying thought
Taught it, I have, a better way to await
Late dreaded hours. As from a deep mouth-breath
Faith seeps across the midriff, drops a balm,
Calming the knotting nerves, so an   I know not
What, a gust or gale intaken,
Awakened has an overseeing eye,
My oldest guide, who serves an endless ought.

This eye - not I - took over thus and taught
Thought mazed in by-way wonderings of late
Fate's mastery - through due release of faith.
Faith (it won't say wherein), whatever nears,
Fears not a whit; let shift as may the date:
Put off a day, a year, a score of years.

Foiled again!
I hear the winds complain,
Back on the old scent.

Dear Breath, swirl in, swirl out!
Before the birth of Doubt
We - you and I - were one,
Who now, alack,
Are both undone!
I am not breath, nor it
Not even where it listeth?
Now is spirit.

That ghost laid
What wraith
Have we instead?

Some sort of T. V. set,
In order, or not,
More or less obeying
More or less relaying
More or less betraying
What?

How know the Source?
Watch the program.

But sets select,
Don't give us what they get.
And I, I must neglect
What else is on tonight.
Of course.

How can I judge a program?
By its own light.

Watch, you say:
This watching's what I am.

*Yet watch you may
And. . .*

Sights are for sight,
 And for hearing, sound;
In the Unapparent
 Their juncture's found.

Not so arrant
 May be the guess:
What makes me *me*
 Is in Timelessness.

As what I see
 Meets what I hear
Neither in the eye
 Nor in the ear;

But as a *Why?*
 Accepts a *So!*
Each taking the other
 That both may know

(As its father and mother
 In a thought combine
Which neither fairly
 Should claim as "mine");

My last year's *me*
 And to-day's *me,* too,
Their predecessors,
 The long queue through,

And their successors,
 Should there be any
(Thanks to penicillin,
 There could be many)

May share - as men
 Share a Form as men -
A particular *Why:*
 Timeless, Amen.

Timeless? Not me!
Not any *me:*
"Me's" bud and bloom and fall
Like any flower,
Being at beck and call,
At bid and bawl
Of every hour.

No, no! I'll see
All I could ever see
Slip suddenly out of sight;
And all my senses
Will totally take flight,
Being but me
And utterly
Without defences.

Meanwhile we
Timelessly
Be
Beyond all chance or changing,
Secretly high
Above that turmoil ranging,
Being, yes, we,
The fitting of the So within the Why.

And as no *me*
Can be
Without its one identifying "I,"
So I, who am beyond,
Must on my "me's" rely,
Being their bond,
Their Why.

These few then of the endless deems
An end can bring
And a beginning set a-wing
I have presented.

Not one of them need be the thing it seems.

Sooth is, if not prevented
By some sad Gorgon stare,
Each can assume
As shifting veils of radiance or gloom
As even can the sky;
As deep a dread is imaged there
And a hope as high.

SCREEN, *n*. and *v.t*. Partition of wood or stone separating without completely cutting off one part of church or room from another, esp. that between nave and choir of cathedral, etc. (ROOD-s); movable piece of furniture designed to shelter from heat, light, draught, etc., or from observation; expression of face or measure adopted for concealment, protection afforded by these; board on which notices are posted; sheet on which lantern or shadow or motion pictures are thrown; body proof against magnetic or electric induction or having property of obstructing such processes, (phot.) lens used to exclude certain forms of radiation; large sieve or riddle for sorting coal, etc., into sizes . . . (cf. OF *escren* prob. f. OHG *skirm* (G schirm) shelter).

Hail, Screen, on which screen-theory may be thrown
While we sit back reflecting! As it grows,
Reflect indeed; for is this our reflection?
What lends it what authority? Who knows
If not this casement opening on - Its Own?

Reflect indeed, for where is the projector,
The lens, the lamp, the current that it's fed,
The film, the camera crew, lights, mike, and script?
Is this whole shooting-match but in my head?
But then, if so, why am I not Director?

Wait now; we've glasses too we should put on,
Lenses fine ground to furnish our correction.
Screens they are too. But screens from what?
Don't ask too soon from what we need protection:
A point will come at which to press that question.

Now through our crystal lunes let's gaze again.
That head you mentioned, what's become of that?
That brain, its centers, circuits, currents, waves. . .
All gone. Dissolved! That Source we would come at
Supplies the brains which picture so the Brain.

An instrument which would depict the Source
Does not produce what baffles it as well.
Nor is a picture what it pictures; though
Picture beyond picture may excel
In picturing the Unpicturable - perforce.

A thought, a feeling, fear, desire, or hope
Must be a sieve that holds back all but Some.
That Some alone's the sum of what is seen
While the sieve's active. How could One come
To see an All? The Many have more scope.

One eye sees - what to one point is shown,
A figure almost flat, depthless, and dull;
Our two eyes join their fields, the sieves unite,
Their lines of sight converge - a rounded, full,
And living image on the Screen is thrown.

Our two ears do the same: what one could hear
By the other's limits finds itself unbound,
The two together in their differing phase
Locate our sound; but not alone through sound:
Reflex eye-searchings orient the ear.

Thus do the senses - no more led to strive,
Named for an omen - make the World of Sense
The model for the Mind: nor less for State.
Its fateful summary of experience:
Consentaneity alone will thrive.

*   *   *   *

Ho, Lovers! Tend your screens! Thereon depend
Your fluctuant worlds - both as to what you see
And still more what you don't: his screen, her veil;
Hers, his - you Curious! Whence secretly
The upkeep of your foe as of your friend.

158

But few don't think each moment's lenses show
Exacter truth, select beyond selection,
"Washed eyes" their warrant for the curse or kiss.
Warier ones, alert through recollection,
The happiest "and the longest journey go."

Meanwhile, what Non-Sense the great Stage displays:
How long will plots and counterplots divert,
Cunning and greed and independence please:
Fear throttling rage and hate inviting hurt
While apprehension every heart dismays.

(These grids without reflect the strains within:
What feet pad round and round that empty room?
What claws scratch on against that shivering door?
What looney prisoner can now assume
No wish denied, the Universe his bin?)

Such on the Screen the current items flung.
The Show goes on. What else we think or feel
Hardly appears. Our glasses and the films
That run through the projector (Reel on! Reel!)
Cut out the stars from which men's hopes are hung.

What's on the Screen depends most on the lenses,
The personal riddle, the single viewer's wearing;
And these are sometimes sold him, sometimes grow
Through induration of his sight and hearing
To mimic the most reputable frenzies.

Normally (and we should scream unheard
"This is not NORMAL; only usual!")
These fluctuating Idols of the Epoch
Are peddled the (sic) individual
- With Sports and Woman's Pages and Crossword -

To warm the gelid spirits, pet and soothe
Into a most companionable snooze
A common, cosy, marketable doze. . .
Since, to inform us, they must first amuse.
(Dear Muses, hence! We've other things to prove.)

So what is on the Screen gets in the screens
Through which we view it. Not utterly (Amen),
Or else our final hope *were* flat despair;
These docilizing lenses crack, and then
We may review anew the might-be-seens.

Recalling our two eyes: how touch and sight,
How taste and smell combine to feed our Senses,
We might, by such example, find a Will,
Consult our Minds, and, switching off pretences,
Gain some idea of how ideas unite.

Cold wars are cyclones spun by rival screens
Through mutual toxication. More than terror
(May still the outcome stay its own outcoming!)
Needs make these maddened Heroes grasp their error,
Learn saner conduct from the in-betweens.

Each of these warring riddles has its merit
Which those with the due blinkers duly see;
Each also is a breeding pit of horrors;
On which, contrariously, they well agree.
But who sees what from both Man might inherit?

How re-design these screens to keep the virtue,
Taking the bugs out, silencing the noise,
Washing the poison out of verbs like "silence,"
Restoring "ordered freedom." What clear poise
That phrase invites: how would such balance hurt you?

*   *   *   *

An older Screen maintains a deeper strife
Round how and why a man should try to live -
Living on Life. Why should we still prolong
The nightmare past, the Living Desert? Give
The credit due to tooth and claw and knife,

And not be still the climax'd beast of prey
Clomb up too high? Honor the ancient shield,
The shining armor of the fighting mind;
But all that's antics now. In this new field
Only an open mind can make its way.

The sick at heart, pain-crystallized, may seek
An earlier peace, may try to lose this world
To win another, buy another life,
Another self; a soul become so meek. . .
O banners, standards, glories all be furled!

Between these two was built the Screen of Screens,
Between the nave and choir: imaged there
May hang Man's fate, at his own hands endured.
Is this how to be human? Praise and prayer?
Terror and pity? To what end by what means?

Eye of the Soul! Here still we have two eyes.
Their vision cannot guide till they combine
To work with other Sensing. Unknown the Source
That tempts, beyond all tempting, the Design,
The tenting, salving, governing Surmise

Words could not utter, may not formulate,
Dare only hint, one to another one:
Before all veils, the Lonely (and therethrough)
Seeks for Itself as Earth veers to the Sun.
And for that search we must be desolate.

I

The properties of the instruments or apparatus employed enter into . . . belong with and confine the scope of the investigation.—*Speculative Instruments,* 114

This picture I take
Is the camera's view,
Not mine: not you.

Change the instrument,
Change the film or screen,
And you, you're seen

Otherwise. So
- You will find -
With my camera mind:

Film varies there
Minute by minute
And you as fast in it.

Where are you then?
Which infra-thought you
Am I now talking to. . .

Ultra-sentiment you?
Among such how to see
How any you can be?

Two seemingly incompatible conceptions can each represent an aspect of the truth. . . . They may serve in turn to represent the facts without ever entering into direct conflict.—Louis de Broglie, *Dialectica*, I, 326

Film's a surface thing
My sense-taken *you*'s
Bring only a skin
Round a void;
Set me to cling
To a vestige as thin.

What though what I sense
Select its takes,
Install, control,
Wreck and remake;
How was it thence
You acquired a soul?

So I might divine
- Create? - my *you,*
Planted in me
Through what you show:
A you only mine
Isolatedly.

This film-thin shot
At substituting
'What A does' for 'A'
Breaks down on you:
Truly you're not
Just 'what you display.'

But why need I tell
You this   who should know

Well enough   how all
Who   take the shadows
For substance   dwell
In this cinema hall.

You've your own *you* too
Which you never touch,
View, taste, or scent,
Though sometimes hear
Saying for you
What you ought to have meant.

That self-same you
- Summoned whence
To the chromosome dance? -
Before your heart beat
Set up a do
Out-reaching chance:

As the CONCEPT here
Has chosen its word
Sheer through the maze
Of the eddying web
Whose balancings clear
Or block its ways.

Two languages:
As of the soul,
As of the cell,
Take it in turn;
In new pages
Each other spell.

Words like 'thoughts' and 'sentiments', equally indispensable to illustrate the diversity of psychical experience, pertain to mutually exclusive situations characterized by a different drawing of the line of separation between subject and object.—Niels Bohr, *Dialectica,* I, 315

Grave news, my dear!
Our mutual thought
Must of all sediment be clear.
For proof: they redefine
The elements of our design!

Here's a formula will build a
High efficiency philtre-filter.

Conversely, to enjoy
The customary fellow feeling,
Each last least germ of thought destroy
As too revealing.

Who may this formula employ
And to what end
And through what schooling
There's no precluding
However finely it intend.

One must draw the line somewhere!

My love, my grief, my fear, my hate,
Dear Fate, do either root in you,
Or I,
Idly driven, idly spy.

Where you end
And I begin
Or any else, in fine,
On such dichotomies depend
There's no one left to draw a line.

V

So must pure lovers' soules descend
T'affections and to faculties
Which sense may reach and apprehend
Else a great Prince in prison lies.
         —John Donne, *The Extasie*

So 'a great Prince in prison lies'
    His servants disaffected:
The affections and the faculties
    Disabled and dejected.

How we could feel, how act:
    The SENTIMENTS - whose rank
Held only by their pact -
    Now have themselves to thank

If the Virtues scowl and skulk,
    While their Helpers helpless droop:
Courage complaining in a sulk
    To Faith, the nincompoop.

Yet between THOUGHT and sense
    The SENTIMENTS have stood
Upholding both, their staunch defence
    Let come what would.

Our task can only be to aim at communicating experiences and views to others by means of language in which the practical use of every word stands in a complementary relation to attempts at its strict definition.—Niels Bohr, *Dialectica*, I, 318

Thought can be a driving rage
    And longing be a mirror;
Each must be both; so stage
    No conflict here, no error.

This line that's no dividing line,
    Dug in, throws all agley;
And they that would that Prince confine
    Can lock him up this way.

Though most who'd separate
    Subject from object so
Have it at heart to liberate
    The known from those who know.

And knowers too from what is known:
    Pure knowing on one hand
And on the other, all alone,
    A sacred *gegenstand*.

But that's not how the show is run:
    This independent mind,
Unkingdom'd, might as well be none -
    As countless Lears find.

And that brave circumstance,
    Untinctured by the eye,
As indistinguishable dance
    Flits vainly by.

Through what we've learned we learn
    And rule through what we rule
Cartesian doubts can swiftly turn
    A sage into a Fool.

So be you not neglectful
    Of incompatibility;
We ARE because we went to school
    To views we could not see.

REFLECTIONS

I

Manifold Motion

Philosophers ador'd the Night, accounting it to have some
great Mystery and Deity in it.—Peter Sterry

Taught, for a moment, by discomfiture,
Gave up and took the treasure to the dump.
Found then, the drainage had to foul the pump.
Give up! Clear out! One endless overture!

Every arrival this; and every departure:
Leaping from rotting strength to iron stump,
With all at stake in each blindfolding jump.
Home-coming this: lighting out at a venture.

Twirl'd up aloft in limitless endeavour
To be sunk back, as soon, below the least.
Caught between choices scissor-set to sever
The toiling thread. From that cocoon released,
Firefly headlighted to annul whatever
Night I flit through: ignorant as a priest.

Content

Poetry lifts the veil from the hidden beauty of the world,
and makes familiar objects be as if they were not familiar;
it reproduces all that it represents, and the impersonations
clothed in its Elysian light stand thenceforward in the
minds of those who have once contemplated them as
memorials of that gentle and exalted c o n t e n t which
extends itself over all thoughts and actions with which
it co-exists.—Shelley, *The Defense of Poetry*

Content? Content. Let be what will
As content this strange Stage fulfill,
Aiding its forms to represent
What may not otherwise be meant;
Let be the Scene that Veil may hide
Of Paradise or parricide;
Calm the supernal Light let shine
Clothing the wreck of the Design.
Under its spare admonishment
We decorate our discontent,
As a perpetual monument,
With better than a coat of paint.

Supplementary Consideration

The Soul within the Body, can I any way compare this to the Reflection of the Fire seen thro' my window on the solid Wall, seeming of course within the solid wall, as deep within as the distance of the Fire from the Wall? I fear, I can make nothing out of it/but why do I always turn away from any interesting Thought to do something uninteresting—as for instance, when this Thought struck me, I turned off my attention suddenly, & went to look for the Wolff which I had missed.—*The Notebooks of Samuel Taylor Coleridge,* #1737

> Not from within the Body
>   Or within a Wall
> The two Fires you would question
>   Would answer your call:
>   "We are not WHERE at all."

> So hints the subtle Window:
>   "I do but half reflect;
> Let by as much as I send back.
>   The Optics you neglect
>   Are of the Intellect."

> Then the Bright Fire, refining:
>   "Beyond a Thought or Fear,
> Self-presenting Spirit,
>   Though mirror'd everywhere,
>   Knows how not to appear."

SEAFARING

Comb and Glass

The life we call blessed is located on a high peak. A narrow way, they say, leads up to it. Many hills intervene, and we must proceed "from virtue to virtue" with exalted steps.—Petrarch on Mont Ventoux

"Uphill all the way,"
It read. . .but
"Going downhill fast, these days,
Yes, running down," they said.

Close up: tangles of tasks in hand.
Far off: a hesitating figure on the sand.

Those billows, all that main,
For Wordsworth, house "a sense sublime. . ."
For Blake, this tumbling life again:
The Sea of Space and Time.
"Though inland far we be,"
Yet, equally, we're all at sea.

Newton's "strange seas of thought"   ?
By routine traffic jammed,
Their lanes queue-ful, their waves taught
Dry, their current cargoes damned.
Who'll now the murex find
Within what reach of mind?

"The Mind, that ocean," sound!
Your psycho-bathysphere
Waits (panting like a hound).
Its intake-sampling gear
Will fish up what is found
In the drowning by the drowned.

Or from Behavior's
Neat correlation curves
Expect new light to win:
A-fumble at the doors
An inner eye observes
Open only from within.

That Eye (we may forget)
Can wake in anyone.
Who'd "sail beyond the sunset"
Must overleap the Sun,
Make ready for "the foolish flight"
In Glaucon's laugh begun.

All set, at last, to win:
Till   three   times   round
Spin our gallant ship and
Three   times   round
Spin we; and
Dizzying down   that Loftiest Land
Close over us the Sea.

Presence

While far below the vast and sullen swell
Of ocean's Alpine azure rose and fell.
                    —Byron, *The Island*

Those tumbling waves,
        The world,
      Breath out, breath in;
      The gain here does begin
The loss that saves.

This very qualm
        The One
      Prescribes, provides.
      This ripple rides
The central Calm.

And though so much
        Beyond
      Our dread, our fear,
      Its threatening were:
Its searing touch

More sharp, more sheer;
        Its bite
      More foul, more fell
      Than any hell
And near. . .and here -

The Calm remains
        Entire;
      In no dismay,
      In clear array,
Supports our pains;

Bears our delights
    As well:
   Our malices,
   Our cruelties,
Our hates and spites;

Restores our wings
    To soar
   To seek to see,
   Unwaveringly,
What timeless Sings.

We, being by
    The Song
   Nearer than near,
Hearing, hear why.

END OF A COURSE

In Memory of Theodore Spencer
4 July 1902—18 January 1949

He and I,
Giving Humanities I together,
Iliad, Old Testament, Phaedo. .I,
New Testament, Paradiso, Hamlet. .he,
Strolled to my room through the open weather.
Full January thaw. Examination weighed,
He turned to go: "The readiness is all!"
Said to the Calendar on the wall,
Stooping to glance at it to see
The date in Spring when we'd be free.
"Earlier than ever!" Rubbing his hands in glee,
Leapt down my steps into the sun.

All done.
He crossed the Yard, waved to a friend,
Looked up a book, then took
A taxi-ride that had no end.

Coconut Grove, Florida
18 *January* 1959

More than affectionately old,
Old clock,
With staid tick-tock,
Blocking out, rounding up
The intangible flow;
Warming-pan pendulum
Sedately swaying;
Minute hand stepping and staying,
Acting, enacting,
Again and ago. . .
After faint hum
You strike:
One. Endless the wait before. . .
Two. But this I especially like:
Three comes sooner and the rest come
Quicker and quicker till the sum
Is told.

Coconut Grove
10 *February* 1959

SEMANTICIST'S DANCE

If I had some ham
I'd have ham and eggs
If I had the eggs. . .
—*Prospector's Day Dream*

It is no ill chance, but right and justice, that has sent
thee forth to travel on this way. Far indeed does it lie from
the beaten track of men. Meet it is that thou shouldst learn
all things, as well the unshaken heart of well-rounded truth,
as the opinions of mortals in which is no true belief at all.
—*Parmenides*

Alone in my field
And the field fine;
More than a field, a world,
And this world mine
(Though less than in the view of Wittgenstein).

Our worlds talk to us,
Talk for us too,
Show what we are to them
And what speaks through
Our worlds; and whether what's said is true.

Tell that to whom though -
Lengthening the tether
Whose pin's never pulled?
Birds of a feather
In these surmisings hardly flock together.

Nothing less human
Than to be devising
Answers to questions
Never arising,
Solvents to sayings none find surprising.

No. But try it,
And: "You must be playing!"
Keep on at it. . .
We become dismaying,
Our fancies common - *lifeline* - sense betraying.

Not though to him who
Against all the chances
Turns his eye hither:
Whose ungovernable glances
Happen on the guess our utterance advances.

What were the odds should
The very unlikeness
Wreck the routine and
- Sheer out of randomness -
Score a full hit on an unknown address?

In most other knowledges
Order's the limit,
Team-work and discipline:
"Every whit does its bit!"
Agreement and Difference! Let's not forget it!

Bright the Satanic Mills,
Not lacking innocence:
James and John Stuart
Lay by pretence,
Lay down the rules of the Wherefore and Whence.

"Generality"
- So say the Schools -
"Breeds Objectivity,
Save for the Fools
Who'd junk the findings Our experience pools!"

Findings! Sweepings!
Droppings of the Mind,
Spoils of the dustpan

To the deep-freeze consigned.
It takes a Herd to think it makes a Kind.

Generality?
Sameness conferred
By what? What pens
All that's occurred,
Or ever will, within the confines of a word?

What binds to its own self?
What selfs each Will?
What makes, say, White
Stay White unchangeable?
What holds things So and makes change possible?

Such questions chase their queues
Would have us know
What makes them them.
But that's as though
A ball within itself itself would stow.

How see oneself?
Reflect: no mirror's skin
Throws back those rays.
And, what though you imagine,
What you descry is not what would be seen.

Be not too sure!
The vacant eye
Some scattering beam
May occupy,
Dream dreams therethrough in princely vanity.

White knows it's White
And keeps White too.
But how am I Myself?
(And Who are You?)
By what clear sign am I to know? (Who knew?

Who knew!) Who now
Slink in adulterine?
Such daimons and such bugs,
Subfusc, feline,
Claim to be me and speak upon my line.

What's speaking now
Saying I may not be
Until - beyond all skill
In this prolixity -
The refluent rays are met to end Obliquity   ?

Ha! Query floating free!   ¿
Bent emblem of all Bend,
Hook of perplexity!
Alone in my field   ?   Perpend!
Not fished out yet. . .   my Friend!

THE STRAYED POET

Ludwig Wittgenstein

How salute you, Dubious Angel,
Proud as the proudest in the race of men,
Battler with the deadliest burden
Self can lay on thought to bind a spell.

How compel (what use else in excelling!)
How overcome (though not a trader's inch you'd yield);
Hide (from yourself?) what well must be concealed;
Earn so a destiny awaits its telling.

Assume Yourself: your selves to duty cowing
By the great Act of vanity maintained,
That old presumption, now to reign unreined,
Reckless of what in all you're disallowing.

Round on round through the long decades of guessing
Against a bosom Jacob who prevailed,
Got off with all the questions duly veiled,
Won out - new named - received the Blessing,

Prospered. His spiritual sons sit in our studies,
Teaching talkers   commonsense,   by screed,
How to cobble a problem when there's need.
Your scions are fewer far - despite those "Bloody" s.

*   *   *   *

Your voice and his I heard in those Non-Lectures
- Hammock chairs sprawled skew-wise all about;
Moore in the armchair bent on writing it all out -
Each soul agog for any word of yours.

Few could long withstand your haggard beauty,
Disdainful lips, wide eyes bright-lit with scorn,
Furrowed brow, square smile, sorrow-born
World-abandoning devotion to your duty.

Such the torment felt, the spell-bound listeners
Watched and waited for the words to come,
Held and bit their breath while you were dumb,
Anguished, helpless, for the hidden prisoners.

Poke the fire again! Open the window!
Shut it! - patient pacing unavailing,
Barren the revelations on the ceiling -
Dash back again to agitate a cinder.

"O it's so clear! It's absolutely clear!"
Tense nerves crisp tenser then throughout the school;
Pencils are poised: *"Oh, I'm a bloody fool!*
A damn'd fool!" - So: however it appear.

Not that the Master isn't pedagogic:
Thought-free brows grow pearly as they gaze
Hearts bleed with him. But - should you want a blaze,
Try prompting!   Who is the next will drop a brick?

Window re-opened, fire attack't again,
(Leave, but leave what's out, long since, alone!)
Great calm; a sentence started; then the groan
Arrests the pencil leads. Round back to the refrain.

*   *   *   *

What withheld, O Will volcanic:
Riven eagle, staring at the Sun?
Sight denied you? Blinded such an One?
What remained you but the drive Satanic?

184

WHAT MAY NOT BE SAID: you could not say it.
Let all language then turn to a game.
(Jacob, go gently, he's coming into aim)
Worth the candle? No. Why now illuminate?

What the stakes though? Still sidereal.
What there is: "The World and Life are One."
Shrivels or grows together all that's done.
Seeing: "The Eye altering alters All."

Blake's Eye, exact. But you in your *Tractatus:*
"The limits of my language mean the limits of my world."
What sets our limits? How were you unfurled?
Where is the Rule assigns to us our status?

"The thinking. . .subject: there is no such thing."
"Metaphysical I" instead: "no part, but limit."
"My world the world is." They much more than fit;
Are one, not two: one single uttering.

So *I* and *my* aren't here our current words,
Live in another language far from ours,
Hardly a language: limitless its powers.
Speech to that WORD - forget not - ill accords.

"Everything that can be said can be said clearly."
Maybe; with what strained sense for *clear* and *say?*
Those other things that can't, alas, must they
Be "shown" - by whom and howsoever dearly?

Those picturing facts *Tractatus* wished at us:
Against the new Rules! Nothing to picture now!
No picturers, no pictures! Jacob who would not bow
Can well insist we take it from him thus.

Instead of mirroring - and, far less, comparing -
Let us observe the Rules - not ours to change!
Or are they? Why not think up a range
Of Rules for Rules: up, up. . .beyond all bearing?

Much turned on who among the YOU s you were.
Some YOU s, it seemed, had wider scope for play.
One YOU, (he limped, that YOU), won *May;*
Others *May not,* for all their zeal and care.

Collector of Blessings, count your gains; earmark
The bleatings; Peniel recall. That face of God
Overcame you not, old trickster, though roughshod
He wrenched your hip, ford-haunting in the dark.

But now you hold the ford, let whom you list,
Pass on the word, taking his name in vain,
Taking the hairy hand, the mask of pain,
The wordlessness that can, so will, insist.

Insist? To whom? The faithful, few but fit;
Or found unfitted - ah, exposed at last,
Void echoers. Beware, poor paraphrast:
Say it *for* me, would you!   That I *don't* permit.

Insisting still on what's so clear and sure,
Say as you may, all, all, must get it wrong:
"Not that at all! Good Heavens!" No words strong
Enough even to hint what you endure.

*   *   *   *

Above these little games a Game there plays
Takes note of "airs" - has much to do with air
(Aeronautical engineers), with the impair,
And some invariants Plato's page displays.

Watching it mutely, an onlooker's neglect
Seemed wiser as well as safer. None could aid.
Much there was here would make the Elect afraid.
Eyes as deject as mine must be suspect.

Fallen to a game, alas, and in despair:
Too heady, too enthralling, such command?
Jacob be given up as deodand.
Let that alone for ever, Prince of the Air.

SILENCES

The Talipot Palm of Ceylon, one of the wonders of the
plant world, grows to be 80 feet high in 40 years, then
flowers, producing 2 tons of bloom and thousands of fruits.
It then dies.—*Notice under a photograph in the David
Fairchild Tropical Gardens, Coconut Grove, Florida*

I

Suppose we meet a silence. While it's clear,
While not a wave checks in along the shore,
While nothing breaks it, not a thought or word,
Not a leaf stirring - where will we be then?

Is it that silence you would choose to hear?
Or our own selves thinking? Ours the floor
Our own selves all the audience: to be heard,
To hear - beyond the reach of men?

Silence, no doubt, 's the ground of utterance,
Pausing its pulses and completing it;
No utterance without. But listen! When,
If ever in the windings of the dance,
To-be-said and *saying* in perfection fit,
Another silence listens: listen again.

The outcome's not the point, those sportsmen say.
The over-all outcome's something else again.
Our outcome, what we've hoped so to achieve,
Could not have been, or done, as we supposed -
Suppose it somehow realized.   We play
Our games; win, lose.   All which would be inane
If even   the uttermost we may conceive
Of less conditional enclosing games   forclosed
A thing.   How ask all that to freeze
An instant and for what! That we may succeed?
In what?   In due accordance with the Way?
In being ourselves? In doing what we please?
In getting but an inkling of our need?
In learning how to hold our peace or pray?

For all such fleetings - figures on a ground -
Let the Giraffe play emblem: none so tall,
Gentle, aloof, free, delicate and calm;
He bears the casting net set in his skin;
Strides like a wave, within those meshes bound;
Lives there unspotted, Captive of the All.
Another image shape: the Talipot Palm
Ending itself for others to begin.

Take and make over. There's no soon or late
In the perpetual. This would still have been
Had our concern kept concert with our powers.
Ground becomes figure: what we would create
Backs down, fades out, gives place to what's between
The lines, the patches; and behind the hours.

WARHEAD WAKES

I

"To prevent surprise destruction an undisclosed number of the planes of any strategic command must today be always airborne, fuelled and equipped for action," the spokesman said.

Over East Anglia
No bluer skies could be
Illumined so with fear
Illimitably.

So over Novgorod
Or elsewhere, where you will,
Calligraphy of God
Suspends the Kill.

The circuits of our hopes as well
Depend - on a common hell.

The flash of nuclear explosions set off at very great altitudes last year blinded rabbits up to 300 miles away, the Atomic Energy Commission disclosed today.—*The Times,* June 16, 1959

Was this carefulness
Beyond excess,
Or just carelessness
Or couldn't care less?

You'd think
This'd make us blink!
It did. The sentence was so bleak
We rabbits have said nothing for a week.

Blink-reflex times are slow: too slow, it's clear,
Think-reflex times far slower; so we fear.

Lenin declared that Any Cook
   - How sure the hope that chose the word -
Ought to be able to govern the state.
   Did Lenin cook? I haven't heard.

Besides, what's cooking? Ham and eggs?
   The soufflé? *Pâté* Aphrodyne?
The accounts? Production curve reports?
   History?   The party Line?

Seek nobler thoughts. Find Lenin's aim:
   To glorify the gifts of men.
Shut up the holocidal shop
   And call us to the Banquet then!

SUCCESS

Of a Promising Student, in Anticipation

A world deep in his debt
Pays interest full - and yet. . .

What need was solaced so?
What lonely fight,
What sacrifices of delight,
What anguish in the long ago?

And what extremities of prayer
Built up what head of longing there,
What hunger for renown
That now he must disown
With apprehensive frown?

And what wry self-distrust
The young hood-winker thrust
Into such coy pursuit?
What bittering snub
Was just enough to stub
And polish such astute
Appraisal of the ropes
That realize such hopes?

By what adroit disguise
Grained in beyond surprise
Did this suave metamorph
This migrant on a whorf
This psyche out of grub,
This pard attired as hind
Leave all the rest behind?

Little sign
Amid such high, benign

Complacency and charm,
Such calm array;
But some quick anger and alarm
Peeking through the bland display
And the alerted eye,
Spying out who deny.

METEMPSYCHOSIS

Tired out from stalking round the empty deck,
A striped hyena in his fetid cage,
Padding about - but not now in a rage.

Long voyage over, is this dock or wreck?
Much set in order, save what matters most.
What can be order in a frightened ghost?

Whatever else there is, I should neglect.
How save what matters most? How compose
Postures agreeable to   what I suppose?

It's been an exercise to recollect
Those flames, ice-spears, extremities of pain
Our terrors planned: gymnasia for disdain.

Or symbols: what the anguished self can do
To its own hopes. What's coming to
The traitor. Those wages! Those rewards!

Who wants to feel rewarded? Sheath your swords,
You guardians of the walls of Paradise!
No doubt long since you did: since we grew wise
Enough, ourselves, to ask what we deserve.

That is so far off that once loomed so near,
Strange to be tasting a familiar fear.

Someone is waiting for me, I observe.

It seems more mirror than a portal here -
Where my receptionist, grown all I see
Rears at me as I rear and I am he.

Some of these click beetles emit a bright light from a portion of their bodies, which leads to the recognition of mate or comrade by sight.—ENCYCLOPAEDIA BRITANNICA, 11th Edition

So. . .so. . .
Old Firefly!
Do you flash and flit by. . .
Quick!
And alone!
(Where once a throng?)
Alone in the Dark,
Under the Forest, overhung;
Although, on high,
The Moon, at full,
O'erflood the Sky.
So now, fleet Spark,
Through Air as thick
And close as Wool,
Flit on: -
Your Flash, this Song.

Flit by the Stem
That leans and turns and lifts
- Displaying them -
Its Galaxy of fans:
Adroop to the Earth's pull,
Afloat on the Air's flow,
Feather'd, aswing
As any wing
As the Breeze shifts.
Now flash and show
Old Scars across the Bark
Where, aeons
Ago,

The undercrown
Dropt down
That the Tree might grow.

Hands up, now
To the Moon:
Quivering Blades
Smooth as Flint
And serried as a Rake!
      But how
- Glint by glint -
Do you sweep up Stars?
      Or do your crisscross Shades
But make
Visible what the strewn
Radiance bars?
      No, no; it's but
The glitter of the Moon
Glancing along
Some glassy Flake.

That skipjack Beetle's flown
Out of the Gloom
Into the Moonflood where
His flashing's no more seen.
It isn't his;
Nor, even, is
The Moon's Serene
Her own.
She needs her Shade
As he his Glade;
As the Palm's Stars
Their Perpendiculars;
But to have been:
Been seen, been known.
By whom?

Coconut Grove, Florida
20-30 *December* 1958

Nature is better dressed than Man.
These various Birds and Fish,
Even the 'gator on his bank,
Can
Make one wish
We people weren't so rank.

And, most, the Humbled One,
Self-fluent, living Stream,
Upon his belly in the dust:
None
Of all seem
In better Taste.

His suiting modest, rich, subdued,
Choice custom drape,
In stripe and weave correct:
Shrewd
For a Shape
So bitterly abject!

He, who originally rolled
"Erect," uplifted high
"His burnish't Neck of verdant
Gold,"
"Crested aloft" and eye
Observant,

Through which the sight of Eve at work
Stooping amid her "Flourie Plat,"
Converting Satan, could
Irk
Evil itself, the Plot forgot:
"Stupidly good";

He whom the Tempter found
("Fearless unfeared he slept."
Why should he watch unwarned?)
And,
Within him crept,
Seized and suborned:

Brer Serpent, never a fool,
"Nor nocent yet" - a friend
To all - how should he know?
Tool
Only and
Punished so!

See now, the fly, the bream,
Bass, cormorant, gar and 'gator
Ravening. Was this all through
Him?
And later
Bikinis too?

Everglades National Park
27 January 1959

Heavens! Against the blue:
Spring!   A day or two
After Fall!   Down swirl'd
The rubbertree's brown leaves.
Before they've curled
Up, Lo!
Mocking the olive's hoary sheen,
The silvery sage young green.
As it were between:

Merita! Merita! Merita! Merita!

Bursts of the Red Bird's paean:

Here! Here! Cheer! Cheer! Cheer!

As for the Empyrean.

> Giddy go!
> Leave sheaves!
> Live so!

Coconut Grove, Florida
February 1959

OVERHEARD

Hark!
Invisible
Loud
Counsel
From the trees!

Syllable-
Clear, clear
As bell,
Will tell
What the proud
Heart
Would still
As lief
Not hear:

"Do what you will,
All said,
All done,
What's won?
What bread?
What bed?
What word?
What's even begun?"

"Believe that thief!
How like a Bird!
Absurd!
All's well!
(Hear! Hear!)
Yes, here
And now
And how!"

"Leaf within leaf,
Well sped!
All's clear!"

"You too,
      Who view,
You too,
      Who woo,
But who to
      Do sue,
Who to?
      Who?"

Magdalene College Garden
June 1959

THE YEARLING SWIFT

Although the yearling swifts do not breed, they frequent
the colonies during the breeding season, selecting holes,
forming pairs and even building nests.—"The Home Life
of the Swift" by David and Elizabeth Lack in *20th Century
Bestiary*, A Scientific American book, Simon and Schuster.

Bygones, begone! They trouble me:
Echoings   from   what used to be.
Study, instead, to soothe the mind,
These ultra-denizens of the wind:
Scarce here, than passed - sped flashing by
On after-images in the eye.

Before these Birds were got or laid
Parents in Africa   fed and played:
Skimming the water's film for drink;
Climbing, higher than you can think,
Screaming up   s p i r a l s leading to
Winging a night-long c y c l e   through;
Falling, as dawn comes w h e e l i n g by;
To snatch a gnat or early fly;
Weaving up North - swung North, the Sun -
Back to the homesite, fought for, won;
Waiting about   till - flap - who's here?
The fellow you went with yester year!
Building anew the nest you built,
All out of airborne   drift   and   silt,
Anything carried by gust or flaw:
Petal or feather or leaf or straw.
Gumming them - wall and flange and floor -
Leaving a drop-hole for your door.

Then, ah then, at the sacred hour
Poised betwixt   dearth and dower
Balanced between   night and day

Out on a brilliant wing of May:
Eight p.m. or six a.m.;
Then the aerial requiem:
Gliding down the cushioning air
Scream together the mating pair.

Two, or three, eggs: what toil and pain;
Chill England hung with mist and rain;
Hardly an insect on the wing:
Five hours of s w o o p i n g but to bring
One bolus back to a gaping bill.
Until, one day when you've caught your fill,
What you've been feeding and fending for
Has quietly tipped through your drop-hole door,
S p r e a d out its wings, unspread before,
O p e n e d its life-time in the air,
Beat it, maybe, to Africa.

Didn't you, once, from a nest so steal?
Better gulp down that needless meal!

See now the yearlings, home again,
African flights enjoyed in vain,
Colony-circling far and near.
What is it now they play at here?

Outcomes, come out! They baffle me:
S a m p l i n g s of what needs must be.

Weal or woe, here we go;
Nothing in the bag to show.
Plash, rash Haberdash, seek a bugaboo!
Who but one comes tumbling to?

There, it's done; lost and won;
Now play 'possum in the sun.
Toss 'em, Haberdash, etc.

Hoo! ha! hoo! Tumble to!
Tumble's not what tumblers do!
Not what, Haberdash, etc.

Who? Ah! Me! Dread to see
Such an one his weird mun dree!
Honey, Haberdash, etc.

Tight and tore; tight no more;
Not a patch on 't as before.
Catch on, Haberdash, etc.

Who must thrive, first connive;
Let the rest just keep alive!
Zest up, Haberdash, etc.

Who would fix, he must mix,
Not go haunting by the Styx.
Flaunting, Haberdash, etc.

Not but Heaven's useful leaven;
Acts as foil to the Deadly Seven!
Toil on, Haberdash, etc.

Soon or late - it can wait -
We'll be shown which is our Gate.
Bone up, Haberdash, etc.

Wet or fine, bant or dine,
Don't forget the countersign.
Get set, Haberdash, etc.

Now and then, if and when,
Celebrate this regimen.
Rate it, Haberdash, seek a bugaboo!
Who, tho' late, comes tumbling to?

Modest harebell, swaying gay,
Honored have you been today:
A Tourist, taken by your grace,
Hailed you "ENZIAN" to your face;
As beside your glance he knelt,
I knew exactly what you felt.

HOPE

To D. E. P. in hospital for a broken hip

My dear: Wales has a slab
Named Hope - a tall, buff, tilting thing.
It listens, these late centuries,
To querulous, lost, impatient lambs
And the ambiguous sheep
Conversing through the mist.
There, leading, one cool Spring,
Rope out, the holds glare ice,
You found your pocket scissors:
                    stab by stab
Picked enough clear, floated on up.
              I keep
A memory of that for other jams:
You immaterialist,
Who know when to persist.

Recall the Epicoun:
Night, welling up so soon,
Near sank us in soft snow.
At the stiff-frozen dawn,
When Time had ceased to flow,
- The glacier ledge our unmade bed -
I hear you through your yawn:
"Leaping crevasses in the dark,
That's how to live!" you said.
No room in that to hedge:
A razor's edge of a remark.

Yes, not less present now than when
You gambolled down that slope,
Shuffling the beech-
Leaves,
Kicking up such a din
We had to talk or walk.

But now is here, and then was then.

Even a dead beech-
Leaf,
Within its javelin head, can glow
As warmly as a peach.

There, there!
It's but a skin,
A skin, a bloom,
So thin it leaves
No room for grief.

Tricks of the visible,
Its sunset show.

From
The Indivisible
All come. And we,
Before the senses were
And after their despair,
Are what no eye can see.

Up hill, down dale. . .
So ran the tale.

We have them in our bones:
Ten thousand miles of stones,
Moraine, débris and scree;
As many, could-be twice,
Over the fissured ice,
The clinging, slippery snows
That of our feet dispose;
As many again, or more,
Beside the torrent's roar,
Within the scented gloom
Or through the sorrowing cwm.

Or by the scythe-worn dell,
And cow-placated swell
Up the redeeming grass
Lifting toward the pass.

Along the ridge itself,
The ridge that earns its pride,
Riven from either side:
Lord of the rift or shelf
Whence the awaiting cliffs
Hang out their 'buts' and 'ifs'
To magnetize the eye
From sweeping round the suspect sky,
That could so soon prevent
Our inexplicable intent.

Or where the driven snow
Invites our steps to show
No fluted, rearing wall,
Or plum'd crest too tall
For our impertinence.

What did we gather thence?
The bootprint in the dust,
The upward roll and thrust,
The limber footfall plunging down,
The axe-head friendly in the palm
Or snug between the sack and arm.
Clutches of delicate fears,
Qualms as the *néant* nears:
Relieved - our summit joys;
Relived - what toys!

All that - Goodbye!
And this has told you why:
Not of all that bereft,
But we, ourselves, have left. . .
Leave that behind.
And not as Fall. . .
Even resigned.

SATIATION THEORY

I

After the great wave lesser waves seem shrunk
To some; to others not. Back here in the womb,
Here in our nearest mock-up, we assume
Under deficiency of waves we're sunk
And kick to be let out. Accordingly:
Those take pain best who shrink fresh waves the most;
Those make best prisoners whose waves least have lost
After - because of - what wild ecstasy?

The extravert, they say, will underrate:
His but to DO - not cultivate the sigh.
Those who grow old with grace don't like life less.
The escape from love's for the smart satiate.
If we might choose, it seems the choice would lie
Between a dodge with pain - and loneliness.

Slung like a spider's web above a void
- Image of frailty, stronger though than steel -
Strings, these, for every pang that you can feel,
For all the tastes in you that can be cloyed.
Tauten or slacken for the testing touch.
Hereabouts the mean is; seek it heedfully,
While a remainder answers faithfully.
Enough's enough; too much can be too much.

Listen! The astonished ear scales down its take.
Look! The insulted eye declines, won't see
As formerly it could. Be not so rough;
Let not your will its own attunement break,
Nor strain the joints of thought; but skilfully
Salute *Enough*.   Little enough's *Enough*.

To what excess you practice what you preach!
A poem can glut or starve. Starve too far,
Pump down too low a vacuum, there you are:
Met by a change of sign. You overreach.
What was too little has become too much,
The want itself has swollen out of bounds,
The silence grown too loud. The change confounds
Presence and absence: they wring you in one clutch.

Living's at least a poem it must dictate:
No cancelling, nor known what it's about:
It balances between Within - Without
Across ten billion axes.   Satiate?
What's been controls how we may take what comes.
Pray, fingers, pray: "Let us not be all thumbs!"

All brightens swiftly; all will soon be clear.
The little lights have vanished, star by star;
Along this shore lingers but Lucifer.
Clear: we were never where we saw we were,
Nor are, nor will be, where we see we are;
Nor far off from it, either; no, nor near.

You make broad day your house;
My mind moves with the bat, the owl, the mouse.

Turn and, in turning, know what's turned about;
What turns you too: the handled and the hand.
Being become the most elaborate top,
(Bare earth's the oldest, simplest, in the shop)
Topmost, we say, who the most understand,
Go spin your yarn beyond the doughtiest doubt.

What's truest should be right;
This beaver industry befits the night.

To spin a clue you do not stand your ground,
Unless that ground's the axis of the spin;
But axes have their cyclic wobbles all,
(The Pole Star wanders, is precessional)
Distinctive vortices worked out within
- Mounted, you say, upon - the daily round.

You make broad day your house;
My mind moves with the bat, the owl, the mouse.

My wobble now salutes your wobble, you;
Yet let's not inconsiderately rejoice
In individualities we gain

215

(Thus to subvert our only suzerain)
By random shrinkage of our scope of choice
Or deprivation of our orbits' due.

What's truest should be right;
This beaver industry befits the night.

Broad day shows more than you may care to see.
It is the night sky opens to the stars.
We obscurantists can pretend, as well.
(Baillie! Where are you off to with that bell!)
More light! And more! Forever! Naught debars
Fact breeding on and on to infinity.

You make broad day your house;
My mind moves with the bat, the owl, the mouse.

Dam up a rivulet to form a pond,
The water well above the lintel mark,
And build within a wolverine-proof Lodge.
(The underwater doorway is the dodge.)
There, as day dazzles, you preserve your dark.
Nibble your store of bark. Let be beyond.

What's truest should be right;
This beaver industry befits the night.

Who would have taught,
Had Plato fabled not,
That HAVE   (no less),
By sly HAVE-NOT beguiled,
In a drunken dream
Begot
Their daemon child?

Untouched, unseen,
This supreme go-between,
And matchmaker,
For lowly and for high,
Must ever in-
tervene
As light must for the eye.

New Moon, uphold
Your phantom of the Old!
That shadowy radiance there
By Earth's vast orb is thrown;
Its glimmer's but
The cold
Reflection of our glare.

Presumably,
No drunken dream could be -
Though HAVE-NOT could
Not dream it otherwise;
In all her craft but see
Humility,
Lit by too great a prize.

Did not HAVE guess
All this, the limitless;
And would he not connive
And cap her guile:
Play the dream part,
Acquiesce
With a secret smile?

Daemon desire,
Unfuelled fire,
Would offer up
Lover and Love:
Not least who most
Aspire
To find them Selves above.

Hunger's Lord still!
Boundless his realm until
His inverse, Agape,
In parity was born
To set up *give* for *get,*
To succor the forlorn,
Fulfil,
As never yet,
As never surfeit will.

BY THE POOL

*In his meditation under the Bo tree, Gotama may
have decided—in love and pity—to teach a doctrine
which would do men good rather than another doc-
trine which few only could follow.*

Not beneath the Bo tree
- Its long-tongued leaves
Poplar-like, a-flutter -
This Buddha sits;
But by a limpid water
Welling by;

Which maybe more befits
Words none will utter
Whoever sigh.

There search-winds of heaven
Twirl an imploring leaf,
Set the whole Tree a-shiver
In glory, in grief:
Beneath, the All-giver
In pity willed
To bind up the Sheaf.

Here by his River
That tumult's stilled.

*Not ours to bind,
That way the sword;
Who lay aside the cord
They alone find.*

Truly inaudible
- Yet to be heard
By the ear of the mind -

The penultimate word
Ultimate ripple.

The still figure
Beyond the flow
Listens, listened
Aeons ago.
Ever a-flutter
Must all words be.

Here is an end.

NOTES

THE SCREENS

select beyond selection:

Sense-perception is the triumph of abstraction in animal experience. Such abstraction arises from the growth of selective emphasis. It endows human life with three gifts, namely, an approach to accuracy, a sense of the qualitative differentiation of external activities, a neglect of essential connections.

> —A. N. Whitehead, *Modes of Thought,* 100,
> quoted and discussed *minutely* in my *How to
> Read a Page.* See, especially, pages 88-94.

The Imagination projects the life of the mind not upon Nature in Sense I, the field of the influences from without to which we are subject, but upon a Nature that is already a projection of our sensibility. The deadest Nature that we can conceive is already a Nature of our making. It is a Nature shaped by certain of our needs, and when we "lend it a life drawn from the human spirit" it is reshaped in accordance with our other needs. But our needs do not originate in us. They come from our relations to Nature in Sense I. We do not create the food that we eat, or the air that we breathe, or the other people we talk to; we do create, from our relations to them, every image we have "of" them.

> —*Coleridge on Imagination,* Chapter VIII.

"Washed eyes":

> The jewels of our father, with wash'd eyes
> Cordelia leaves you: I know you what you are.

> —*King Lear,* I, i, 271-2.

"and the longest journey go":

> it is the code
> Of modern morals, and the beaten road
> Which those poor slaves with weary footsteps tread,
> Who travel to their home among the dead
> By the broad highway of the world, and so
> With one chained friend, perhaps a jealous foe,
> The dreariest and the longest journey go.

> —Shelley, *Epipsychidion,* 153-9.

Cf. *Longest Journey* by E. M. Forster.

Or else our final hope were *flat despair:* from William Empson, "Rolling the Lawn," 11. 1-2.

> You can't beat English lawns. Our final hope
> Is flat despair.

This whole poem has a further debt to acknowledge to his "This Last Pain":

> All those large dreams by which men long live well
> Are magic-lanterned on the smoke of hell;
> This then is real, I have implied,
> A painted, small, transparent slide.

Living on Life:

> in this earthly frame
> Ours is the reptile's lot, much toil, much blame,
> Manifold motions making little speed,
> And to deform and kill the things whereon we feed.
>
> —Coleridge, *Psyche*

COMPLEMENTARY COMPLEMENTARITIES

this cinema hall: See *The Practical Cogitator or The Thinker's Anthology,* selected and edited by Charles P. Curtis, Jr. and Ferris Greenslet, Houghton Mifflin Co., 1953, p. 553.

The next piece is from the *Republic.* It has been very freely done into English by one of the editors. The analogy of the movie instead of Plato's complicated apparatus of shadows in a cave cast by images carried by men hidden by a wall, etc., is not his own. Francis M. Cornford refers to it in a footnote . . . We understand that it was Frank C. Babbitt's.
  Let me offer you an analogy. Suppose a race of men who were born and brought up all their lives in a movie, who have never taken their eyes off the screen. All they have ever seen are the pictures, and all they have ever heard, except each other, is the sound track. That, and only that, is their world. . . .

As the CONCEPT *here: Conceive* (a. OF. *conceveir, -oir:* -L. *concipere.* The primary notion was app. 'to take in and hold'; cf. CATCH.) See OED and epigraph to V, below.

224

So must pure lovers' soules descend
T'affections and to faculties
Which sense may reach and apprehend
Else a great Prince in prison lies.

The affections and the faculties: These are the receptive and the active sides of the "spirit" (θυμός). "The helpers are as it were dogs subject to the rulers who are as it were shepherds." *Republic,* 440D.

SEAFARING

I

Comb and Glass:

> One Friday morn when we set sail
>   And our ship was far from land,
> We there did meet a fair pretty maid
>   With a comb and a glass
>   in her hand, her hand, her hand,
> With a comb and glass in her hand.

> *While the raging seas did roar,*
>   *And the stormy winds did blow,*
> *While we jolly sailor-boys were*
>   *up and up aloft. . .*

Then three times round did our gallant vessel. . .

"a sense sublime. . .":

>   a sense sublime
> Of something far more deeply interfused,
> Whose dwelling is the light of setting suns
> And the round ocean. . .

> *—Tintern Abbey*

> Hence in a season of calm weather
>   Though, inland far we be,
> Our souls have sight of that immortal sea
>   Which brought us hither

> *—Intimations*

this tumbling life again: See Kathleen Raine, "The Sea of Time and Space," *The Journal of the Warburg and Courtauld Institutes,* Vol. XX, Nos. 3-4, 1957.

Newton's "strange seas of thought":

> And from my pillow, looking forth by light
> Of moon or favoring stars, I could behold
> The antechapel where the statue stood
> Of Newton with his prism and silent face,
> The marble index of a mind for ever
> Voyaging through strange seas of Thought, alone.

—The Prelude (1850),
III, 58-63.

their waves taught/Dry:

It is, in fact, nothing short of a miracle that the modern methods of instruction have not yet entirely strangled the holy curiosity of enquiry; for this delicate little plant, aside from stimulation, stands mainly in need of freedom.

—Albert Einstein

"The Mind, that ocean":

> Meanwhile the Mind, from Pleasure less,
> Withdraws into its happiness:
> The Mind, that Ocean where each kind
> Doth streight its own resemblance find;

—Marvell, *The Garden*

That Eye:

For the absolute good is the cause and source of all beauty, just as the sun is the source of all daylight, and it cannot therefore be spoken or written; yet we speak or write of it, in order to start and escort ourselves on the way, and arouse our minds to the vision: the vision itself is the work of him who hath willed to see.

—Plotinus, *Ennead,* VI, 9, 4. A paraphrase made by Robert Bridges: *The Spirit of Man,* 69.

Who'd "sail beyond the sunset":

> The lights begin to twinkle from the rocks;
> The long day wanes; the slow moon climbs; the deep
> Moans round with many voices. Come, my friends,
> 'Tis not too late to seek a newer world.
> Push off, and sitting well in order smite
> The sounding furrows; for my purpose holds

To sail beyond the sunset, and the baths
Of all the western stars, until I die.

—Tennyson, *Ulysses*

"*the foolish flight*": See *Inferno*, XXVI, 112-42. Ulysses, from within "the ancient flame," is speaking:

"Oh brothers!" I said, "who, through a hundred thousand perils are so far West, to this short vigil of your senses which remains, do not deny a trial—beyond the Sun—of the unpeopled world. Consider from what seed you come: you were not made to live like animals but to follow virtue and knowledge."
My companions I so sharpened, with this short speech, for the voyage, that hardly then could I have held them back; and, turning our poop to the morning, of our oars we made wings for the foolish flight.
. . . There appeared a mountain, hazy with distance, and seemed so lofty that I had never seen a higher. Happy were we, but soon in grief when a whirlwind from that new world struck our ship. Three times it made her spin amid the waters; at the fourth up rose the poop and down went the prow—as it pleased Another—till the sea was closed above us.

Glaucon's laugh: Ἄπολλον, ἔφη, δαιμονίας ὑπερβολῆς! *Republic*, 509B-C, a passage quoted in *Goodbye Earth*, p. 58. Dante and Tennyson contrive, between them, a powerful springboard or "hypothesis" for the foolish flight—in the closing words of Mackenna's translation of the *Enneads* "liberation from the alien that besets us here . . . the passing of solitary to solitary."

SEAFARING

II

Of ocean's Alpine azure rose and fell:

the closing line being probably the best concerning the sea yet written by the race of sea-kings.

—Ruskin, "Fiction, Fair and Foul," III.
Works, XXXIV, p. 333.

Restores our wings:

Let us now ask why the soul loses her wings. Something like this: the wing is of bodily things most akin to the divine, by its natural func-

227

tion soaring aloft and carrying that which is heavy into the upper regions where the gods live. The divine is beauty, wisdom, goodness and the like; and by these the wing is nourished and grows; but when fed upon evil and foulness and the opposite of good it wastes away. . . .

A human soul may pass into the life of a beast, or pass again from a beast into a man. But the soul which has never seen the truth can never pass into human form. For a man must have intelligence of universals. . . . This is the recollection of those things which our soul once saw when it journeyed with God—when regardless of that which we now say exists, she raised her head up towards true being. And therefore the mind of the philosopher justly has wings for he is always, as far as he is able, in communion by recollection with those things through communion with which God is divine.

—*Phaedrus,* 246, E; 249, B, C.

SEMANTICIST'S DANCE

Line 5: Ludwig Wittgenstein, author of *Tractatus Logico-Philosophicus* and *Philosophical Investigations.* Impassioned, arrogant, apart, and of convulsive bearing, his students often acquired from him a syndrome of mannerisms which I thought might be named Saint Wittgenstein's dance.

THE STRAYED POET

bosom Jacob: See *Genesis* 32:24-30.

screed: 1) a fragment, cut or torn or broken from a main piece; 2) a lengthy discourse or harangue.

How to cobble a problem:

In comparison with the other arts, philosophy, even in its present low estate still enjoys higher prestige which attracts many unfitted for it. . . . Aren't they just like some little bald-headed tinker who has come into money, been let out of prison, had a good wash at the baths and has got himself up to be married to his master's daughter?

—*Republic,* 495.

WHAT MAY NOT BE SAID: "Whereof one cannot speak, thereof one must be silent." *Tractatus Logico-Philosophicus,* 7.

"The World and Life are One": Tractatus, 5.621.

"The Eye altering alters All": William Blake.

"The limits of my language. . .": Tractatus, 5.6.

228

"*The thinking. . .subject. . .*": *Tractatus,* 5.631.

"*Metaphysical I*". . . : *Tractatus,* 5.641.

"*Everything that can. . .*": *Tractatus,* 4.116.

Be "shown": Tractatus, 4.121. "That which expresses *itself* in language, *we* cannot express by language. *Tractatus,* 4.1212: "What *can* be shown *cannot* be said."

Those picturing facts: Tractatus, 2.1 "We make to ourselves pictures of facts." 2.223: "In order to discover whether the picture is true or false we must compare it with reality."

Above these little games:

May we not conceive each of us living beings to be a puppet of the Gods, either their plaything only, or created with a purpose—which of the two we cannot certainly know? But we do know that there are cords which pull the puppets in this way or that . . . and herein lies the difference between virtue and vice. Among these cords there is one which every man ought to grasp and never let go, but pull with it against the rest: the gentle and golden cord of reason. . . .

—Plato, *Laws,* 644E.

as deodand: A thing to be given to God: specifically in English Law, a personal chattel which, having been the immediate occasion of the death of a person, was forfeited to the Crown to be applied to pious uses.

Let that alone:

> For it cost more to redeem their souls
> So he must let that alone for ever.
>
> —*Psalm* 49: 8.

SILENCES

Compare:

And Nature, asked why it brings forth its works, might answer if it cared to listen and to speak:
"It would have been more becoming to put no question but to learn in silence just as I myself am silent and make no habit of talking. And what is your lesson? This: that whatsoever comes into being is my

229

vision, seen in my silence, the vision that belongs to my character who, sprung from vision, am vision loving and create vision."

—Plotinus, *The Enneads,* translated by
Stephen MacKenna, III, 8, 4.

WARHEAD WAKES

The tracks left by these high-flying jets have a doubleness that the double ells in the lines resemble.

COURT OF APPEAL

the Humbled One:

And the LORD God said unto the serpent, Because thou hast done this, cursed art thou from among all cattle and from among every beast of the field; upon thy belly shalt thou go, and dust shalt thou eat all the days of thy life:

—*Genesis,* 3:14.

He, who originally rolled:

> not with indented wave,
> Prone on the ground, as since, but on his reare,
> Circular base of rising foulds, that tour'd
> Fould above fould a surging Maze, his Head
> Crested aloft, and Carbuncle his Eyes;
> With burnisht Neck of verdant Gold, erect
> Amidst his circling Spires, that on the grass
> Floted redundant: pleasing was his shape,
> And lovely,

—*Paradise Lost,* IX, 496-504.

"Flourie Plat":

> Such Pleasure took the Serpent to behold
> This Flourie Plat, the sweet recess of *Eve*
> Thus earlie, thus alone; her Heav'nly forme
> Angelic, but more soft, and Feminine,
> Her graceful Innocence, her every Aire
> Of gesture or lest action overawd
> His Malice, and with rapine sweet bereav'd
> His fierceness of the fierce intent it brought:
> That space the Evil one abstracted stood

230

From his own evil, and for the time remaind
Stupidly good,

—*Paradise Lost,* IX, 455-65.

He whom the Tempter found:

> through each Thicket Danck or Drie,
> Like a black mist low creeping, he held on
> His midnight search, where soonest he might finde
> The Serpent: him fast sleeping soon he found
> In Labyrinth of many a round self-rowld,
> His head the midst, well stor'd with suttle wiles:
> Not yet in horrid Shade or dismal Den,
> Nor nocent yet, but on the grassie Herbe
> Fearless unfeard he slept: in at his Mouth
> The Devil enterd, and his brutal sense,
> In heart or head, possessing soon inspir'd
> With act intelligential; but his sleep
> Disturb'd not, waiting close th' approach of Morn.

—*Paradise Lost,* IX, 179-91.

BONE FOR THE DOG

Bone for the Dog: to the tune of "Knick-knack, paddy wack, give a dog a bone."

HOPE

"Leaping crevasses in the dark . . .":

We realized, with something of a shock, as we scampered up the last few yards to the summit, that dusk was filling the vast trough of the Otemma Glacier. We should have to move very quickly indeed if we were to get off our mountain by nightfall.

Unfortunately the map was very sketchy and thick masses of evening mist were obscuring the view just where we most needed to see clearly. The little Upper Chardonney Glacier seemed to offer the quickest way down, but not till we were on its slopes did we discover that it was scored, under a soft coverlet of new snow, with an endless series of large crevasses. We charged as fast as the crevasses would allow down the glacier, hoping vehemently that each chasm we crossed in the misty growing darkness would prove the last.

Crevassed glaciers *à deux* are always anxious going. In darkness they become a nightmare. I, as the lighter and presumably the more easily

231

fished out, went ahead. I do not know how near I came to going into some abyss. Again and again I seemed to be crawling on all-fours across frail snow-bridges, sounding with my axe in a wet, invisible, yielding, substanceless mush and almost despairing of finding solid ground. Only the knowledge that a night actually on the ice would be a very serious business drove us on from one risky passage to another. The whole thing had become unreal, like a dream, by the time the glacier smoothed out and we could creep, now in complete night, down the final ice—to find ourselves on the edge of abrupt cliffs of glacier-worn rocks. Our last candle was almost burnt out and it was obvious that we could go no further.

—*Climbing Days* by Dorothy E. Pilley, p. 242.

"*THE TEMPORAL THE ALL?*"

I have used one of Hardy's titles to an aim the opposite of his.

RESIGN! RESIGN!

Our inexplicable intent: climbers are often uncommunicative with regard to any first ascent or new route they may have in mind.

SATIATION THEORY

the great wave:

Satiation may indeed prove to be the mechanism of tolerance in that an intermittent bigger wave of pain causes subsequent pain to be perceived as less intense. If this is so, high satiability would be a handicap in a situation involving starvation of sensation, as in sensory monotony or deprivation.

—"Pain Sensitivity, Sensory Deprivation, and Susceptibility to Satiation," by Asenath Petrie, Walter Collins, Philip Solomon, *Science,* December 5, 1958.

nearest mock-up: a tank-type respirator is used in such experiments on deprivation.

The extravert, they say: "the more extraverted the personality the greater his susceptibility to satiation." See H. J. Eysenck, *The Dynamics of Anxiety and Hysteria.*

232

EROS AND AGAPE

Had Plato fabled not: See *Symposium,* 202-03.

"What then is Eros?" I asked. . . . "He is a great spirit (δαιμον) and like all spirits intermediate between divine and mortal. . . ." "And who," I asked, "was his father and who his mother?" "The tale," replied Diotima, is long, but I will tell you. When Aphrodite was born, there was a feast of the gods and Plenty, son of Metis, was present. When the feast was over, Poverty came to the doors begging. Now Plenty, who was overcome with nectar (there was no wine as yet) went into the garden of Zeus and fell heavily asleep. Poverty, being so poor, plotted to have a child by him. So, lying down by his side, she conceived Eros.

To set up give *for* get: Compare Anders Nygren, "Eros is a desire of good for the self. Agape is a self-giving," *Agape and Eros,* Part I, p. 165. See also *How to Read a Page,* pp. 152-56.

BY THE POOL

The penultimate word,
Ultimate ripple:

The last word is silence. Compare Note to "Silences."

TOMORROW MORNING, FAUSTUS!

*An
Infernal
Comedy*

The categories in terms of which we group the events of the world around us are constructions or inventions. The class of prime numbers, animal species . . . squares and circles: all these are "inventions" and not "discoveries." They do not exist in the environment.

—*A Study of Thinking,* BRUNER, GOODNOW, and AUSTIN

DRAMATIS PERSONAE

SATAN: *elderly, tired, distinguished Personage; Chairman of the Board*

BEELZEBUB: *harassed Executive; President*

MOLOCH: *vigorous brimstone General*

BELIAL: *elegant, dissolute Don*

MAMMON: *cultivated Financier*

SOPHIA: *Clerk of the Board, Wisdom Herself*

LORD FAUSTUS

Spoken by Marlowe's Faustus in Scarlet and Bonnet

I Marlowe's Faustus am, come back to tell
All here this truth: I never went to Hell.
All that was painted devils—bugaboo meant
To show me up as Hell-bound and Hell-bent.
Bent I was, true; could never "have grown full straight";
To be that serious was not my fate.
I was a grimly joke—I couldn't find
One jot of purpose in my tittling mind
So had to play with toys: with hopes and fears
You up-to-dates get through in preschool years.
This Doctor's rig—how should a Fool be dressed?—
It was the salt and pepper in the jest.
Fair Science, though, has learnt a thing or two;
To laugh at Doctorates today won't do.
Watch my successor now: he's off to Hell.
What happens there is for the play to tell.

Board Room of the Futurity Foundation, Inc. A large table with seats for five facing the audience. A separate table for the Clerk.
FIENDS *enter in any unexpected ways. For example, by suddenly stepping out from behind black screens placed behind their chairs.*

Enter MAMMON *and* MOLOCH.

MAMMON:
Morning Moloch!

MOLOCH:
                 Morning Mammon! It's
A good thing you and I, at least, have got
Some sense of time.

MAMMON:
          And timing.

MOLOCH:
             That's just it!
And timing. Haven't you noticed, Mammon?

MAMMON:
          I certainly have!

MOLOCH:
Now that we've become a Foundation.

MAMMON:
         Nobody cares.

MOLOCH:
Except you and me.

MAMMON:
Except you and I, Moloch.

MOLOCH:
         Except you and me.

MAMMON:

Nobody except us ever arrives on time.

Enter BELIAL *and* BEELZEBUB. MAMMON *and* MOLOCH *pay no attention to them whatever.*

BEELZEBUB:

You know, Belial, I wouldn't wonder . . .

BELIAL:

I was just thinking the very same thing, Beelzebub.

BEELZEBUB:

I knew it, of course.

BELIAL:

Why not!

BEELZEBUB:

I'd rather say: "Why."

BELIAL:

You mean . . . ?

BEELZEBUB:

Yes, Why.

BELIAL:

There's a reason Why?
Don't you remember that good old song that went . . .

Sings slowly with viperish malice.

Take a goody good look
In the goody good book
There's a goody good reason Why!

BEELZEBUB:

I remember your writing it. Those were the good old days.

BELIAL:

The good old days before we were a Foundation.

BEELZEBUB:

Before we were a Foundation.

Enter SOPHIA.

BELIAL:

Good Morning, Sophy.

SOPHIA:

Good morning, Belial!

BEELZEBUB:

Do you know if Satan's had . . .

SOPHIA:

He's on his way.

MOLOCH:

I hope this time he isn't going to keep us waiting.

Enter SATAN.

SATAN:

All Present.
Then we may as well get started.

They all take their seats, SATAN *central in the Chair; on his right,* MAMMON *and* BELIAL; *on his left,* BEELZEBUB *and* MOLOCH; SOPHIA, *apart at her table facing them.*

SATAN (*putting on a lightly senile mood*):

Well, gentlemen, I need perhaps not take
A lot of time (although, no doubt, we've plenty)
Telling you what this meeting . . . er . . . is for:
A General Epochal Meeting, I observe.
The Clerk! Please note—although it's on this Notice
As all of you, of course, have seen. There has
Been some delay—not inappropriate,
I may perhaps remark: *epoche,* delay;
Epi, upon: *echo,* I hold. Right enough,
Don't you think, before an epoch ends
And a new age begins? (*Stretches and suppresses a yawn.*)
I rather wonder,
Sometimes, if we all of us realize
How serious these decisions of ours may be?
Yes, Belial?

BELIAL:

A slight point, Master: nowise a correction
But a clarification! Am I wrong

In thinking that an epoch is a *point*
To and from which a period is dated
And not itself a period at all—
Except, of course, as a full stop is one?

SATAN:

Very much to the point, Belial, I must say.

BELIAL:

And isn't it ἐπέχειν here rather than *echo?*

SATAN:

I'm sure you're right.

BELIAL:

                     It makes a difference.

SATAN:

I'm sure it must do. Won't you tell us how?

BELIAL:

This long delay there's been complaint about,
This holding back and putting off again,
This prudence some have called "procrastination,"
Others "irresolution," milder terms,
As we all know too well! "Sentiment,"
"Softheartedness," "Humanitarianism,"
Even "Loving-kindness" we have had to bear.
And why? Because we have waited, waiting on,
Watching for the exact point—the turning point—
To come

MOLOCH:

               In my opinion, it's long past already.

BELIAL:

Ever the same sweet Moloch! rough and ready!

MOLOCH:

Ready, maybe. As a soldier, I can say
You never are, you cannot be, too ready.
But rough? I hope not. No. A decent margin
Within that, the pin point! Press hard where you choose!
Exact.

(Demonstrates by dropping a paper clip like a bomb.)

242

MAMMON:

Your two World Wars, for example, so precise,
So economical, so inexpensive!

SATAN:

Gentlemen! It might be easiest
If we became a little bit more formal.
May I call, formally, on our President,
And after him on the Vice Presidents in turn,
To present appreciations of our whole position?
And as your Chairman, Chairman of the Board,
—Mammon and Moloch will, I know, understand—
May I suggest questions and necessary comment
Be either postponed or addressed here to the Chair?
Beelzebub.

BEELZEBUB:

Glad indeed. Make a few remarks.
Afraid—after all this on pin points and precision—
Necessary vagueness.

MOLOCH:

Could you not ask him, sir, to speak more clearly?
I can't bear vagueness.

SATAN (*to* BEELZEBUB):

Moloch's a little
Hard of hearing; he can't hear you.

BEELZEBUB:

Of course!
Sorry Moloch! Well, as I was saying,
What little can be said, can't be said clearly.
It isn't clear itself, at most, not yet,
I rather doubt if ever it can be clear.
When it seems clear, so far, there's nothing in it
Or else we were not looking. We all know
Our Moloch's ancient taste for metaphysics
—*Ultra*physics now perhaps a better term—
Well, seeing *isn't* believing; seeing's finding
And we don't find, I trust, what isn't there!
So my report cannot be very lucid

Nor even brief, if brevity were our aim.

Some time ago, our Intelligence advising,
We placed, you will recall, a certain Faust . . .

BELIAL:

I have, I fear, a serious question for the Chair.

SATAN:

Yes, Belial, what is it?

BELIAL:

The President said FAUST. I call him FAUSTUS.
Is it the self-same man we are talking of?

Up front appears FAUSTUS *in his study sitting at a card table covered with papers. Behind him is a bare blackboard. He is about as far from* SOPHIA *as she is from the* FIENDS. *She turns to regard him. The* FIENDS *black out.*

FAUSTUS:

This interview's not easy. It's with some
Should know me well, but don't at all, I see:

FAUSTUS *scans imaginary faces of the* FIENDS *as if they were before him.*

Wide-eyed and smiling, else expressionless,
Companions not exactly eager to agree
Or in the mood to let me strike them dumb.

Shrugs his shoulders.

No good forecasting even in the round
What they will, or what I may, have to say;
Best leave all to the moment and the whim,
Trick out such ultimate business as a play
You improvise in, free to shift your ground.

Routine vapidities (leisurely warming up
For a snatch take-off) we'll trundle round.

With hand on table imitates plane taking station on runway.

No seat belt though, merely a cigarette.

Takes one.

Is it up to me to get us off the ground?
And what emotion's best as a stirrup cup?

Light on SOPHIA.

SOPHIA:
My serious Faustus thus prepares to die.
Worldly affairs wound up, his ignorant soul
Would plot her course by my inclining eye
Then most, when most; under her own control,
She seeks to be herself, as I am I:
A part reflecting, in herself, the Whole.

FAUSTUS (*addressing imaginary interlocutors*):
Contract? There was a Letter of Agreement.
I have my copy here—

Taking out letter.

                    not signed in fire,
Brimstone, or blood, nothing so bizarre.
To lay down firm the bounds of all desire
Black, lost-forever ink's my instrument.

Lays letter down and addresses imaginary FIENDS.

What breach on my part? None you dare allege
Offsets your total failure to conform!

Pauses and takes letter up.

Better reread in full, refer, recall,
Take bearings in this lull before the storm
Sound calmly now for reefs, feel out my edge.

Here is the bargain:

Reads (and with repetitions).

                  "If they (or IT, through them)

Can tell, reveal, teach me, whatever way,
What I require to know (give me that power)
I'm to be theirs entire, my own SELF pay
As compensation full. . . . Any stratagem,

Device, contrivance, practice, ruse, disguise,
If used by either party for instruction,
—To teach or learn, explore, assay, try out:
That being the key objective of the action—
To be legitimate, not otherwise."

Very bad drafting! I forget now who
Put in which phrases; who hoped which clumsiness
Might give the taken-aback air room at need,
Who didn't care to note where carelessness
Could benefit the adversary too.

Benefit me perhaps. Or all of us?
They haven't taught, I haven't learnt a thing
Since that exalted hour when I called
And they responded: my con*ject*uring
Turned conjuring—three letters less of fuss!

Getting up and writing on blackboard. He is in high spirits.

CONJECTURING
CONJ   URING

E C T an ectomy indeed!
No append*ect*omy that! No knowing yet
What I lost or won by it. DISCOVERY
Gave place then to INVENTION. Don't forget
To what this make-believing was to lead.

They were to teach: I gave them ample powers;
I was to learn: I gave that all I had.
And nothing's happened. Everything's the same.
Inoperative the immitigable hours!
I know no more than then of good or bad.

246

As Faustus' study blacks out the lights go to SOPHIA *while she speaks and then take in the Board Meeting.*

SOPHIA:

When all have known—whatever else they could
Or could not know—have all at least known this,
Their trick of sorting out their bad from Good,

My sutler Faustus can't but take amiss
His fiends' incompetence, and well he should.
He's too near now. His homing echo off,
Distance receptors dead, he's in the trough.

As the Board Meeting returns, BELIAL *repeats his last speech.*

BELIAL:

The President said FAUST. I call him FAUSTUS.
Is it the self-same man we are talking of?

SATAN:

Beelzebub.

BEELZEBUB:

The same. And very much *not* the same, alas!
I am much indebted to my admired friend, Belial,
Who points his finger neatly to the switches
For all our mazy troubles. What's this FAUST
Or FAUSTUS? Settle that, all's clear.
I mean we then could shape a policy.
Till then, this Board itself, our corporate Will,
Must be at variance; our deepest grief,
The heart pang of our woe, taproot, and top,
Is our own lack of unity; and Man,
That bare chameleon, we don't yet know how,
Reflects our differences, might be an image
Thrown, flung, cast, molded on or in the void
Of us ourselves.

MOLOCH:

                    Impudent snake!
Better let me scotch it again and then
I won't say our little darling won't be maimed.

247

MAMMON:

Mr. Chairman! Doubtless our brother Moloch
Was addressing you. May I remark in turn
We have ourselves to serve. These fluctuations,
As Beelzebub sagaciously observed,
Reflect—in ways not fully understood—
Our own economy. Put it at the least:
He is an Index, a useful Index of our state.
Take up our Moloch's tender, his suggestion,
Let him scotch Man again—not to say scorch—
And where might we be then? If you would study
My graphs (I have them in my Office, should you wish)
You'll see enough to make even Moloch cautious.

BELIAL:

If I . . .

SATAN:

Yes, Belial?

BELIAL:

May take this further . . .
I'd like to ask what really is our object?
What do we hope to get through this Faustus after all?

MOLOCH (*interrupting*):

I'd like to ask what Intelligence reports
Of how our Faustus now is looking forward
To our little talk tomorrow. (*Rubbing his hands.*)

BEELZEBUB:

Thank you, Belial.
That takes us back to where we were before
You raised your serious question. We use,
I was saying, this Faustus as a *sound:*
Not only as plummet or lead to attempt to fathom
Or bring up samplings from what's called the bottom,
To search out cavities, vacuities, and hollows.
"To know your enemy," the old maxim goes,
"Know where he is ignorant as well as knowing."
Faustus is NOT our enemy, I need hardly say,
If Moloch will permit me. We are told,

248

He is made in the image of his maker. But
Let us no rash extrapolations risk.
His knowledge should—if he's inspired—reveal;
But not his ignorances.

BELIAL:

                              If the Chair . . .
This image business has me a bit confused.
Beelzebub has made him out our image
Likewise his maker's, as he just now recalled.
For Mammon, he's that potent thing an Index,
Reflects our credit, almost is ourselves.
I rather wonder if this conjurer,
This changeling, this chameleon,
Who feeds on air, as the old stories have it,
This impresario, this illusionist,
Isn't acting up even on Mammon's graphs
To get himself more purchase. How much, I ask,
Is Faustus in on all this image stuff?

SATAN:

Not to add to these uncertainties,
These emptinesses swirling in this void,
I've sometimes taken Faustus as a blueprint
For some sort of new model of ourselves!

Spotlight on SOPHIA. FIENDS *black out.*

SOPHIA:

A part reflecting in herself the whole
Blueprint for a paradigm of conceiving:
In egg or work alike in-built the goal.

As she speaks she moves to stand behind Satan's chair.

These fiends of Faustus in their project weaving:
Fiend trivial (*pointing to* MAMMON)
            dull (*pointing to* BEELZEBUB)
    fantastical (*pointing to* BELIAL)
        or fell (*pointing to* MOLOCH)
Entangled in a cause past their retrieving,

Returns to her own table; FIENDS *are lit again.*

To wreck a universe re-create a soul.

MAMMON:

May I suggest we go on with the Report!

BEELZEBUB:

Willingly! Mindful of much of this
Here so far mentioned, we wrote this Faustus
A Letter of Agreement. Here it is.
I doubt not all your memories retain
Exactly its provisions. The main intent
Was to explore precisely how his lights—
Reflections, as we've said, of a light elsewhere—
Would apprehend and analyze its terms.

BELIAL:

You mean that Letter is our crystal ball
Our prism to sort out, split him like a spectrum;
Pry out, pry into all his modes of being. . . .

BEELZEBUB:

And ours as well, maybe? But let's remember
This isn't optics. It's biology.
It's Faustus' selves we are interested in viewing.
His styles of make-up, you might say, make-believe.
To gather these we had to implant a germ,
Having prepared a culture. We fed it well
And watchfully, and have developed thus
A speculum, so term it, which can yield
Whatever sample insights you may wish
Me to exhibit.

MAMMON:

"Fed it well," you say
May we hear more about this nourishment,
This pabulum for insight? Maybe we,
Ourselves—forgive me, Belial—
Might be the better for a dose of that?

Light on SOPHIA *only. As she speaks, her lines appear on the
large white Screen that hangs over the Board Room table like*

a sound reflector. The FIENDS *freeze into immobility as light leaves them.*

SOPHIA AND SCREEN:
What's said through me through me becomes devote:
Given and given up, its end attained,
Not to be played with more. My words denote
The limits of your license to amend.
What else is yours. Know that mind cannot think
Beyond. Its offering it must still subtend
For all its accurate stepping at the brink.

The Screen goes blank. Light and animation return to the
FIENDS.

SATAN:
If you should so desire, we can have shown
Upon the Impending Screen for all to gaze at
The substance of that course, the nutriment,
With the digestive processes employed,
The assimilations, and the excrement.
Recall the advice I gave Man: "Know thyself!"
That rare advice I gave the fool at Delphi,
"Man, know thyself!"—much good may it have done him!
It was to know all this, inseparably, entire;
But privately: knower secluded with his knowledge.
What's on that Screen is monitored in heaven.
We have some secrets still, at least, you trust so.

BELIAL:
Foul souls have called *us* heaven's excrement.

MOLOCH:
One of them, I think, had Belial in mind.

SATAN:
My followers, companions, friends of old
And fellows then—these late divisions,
These strains within our body, reappear
Perforce within this Instrument of ours.
If we project the history of Faustus,
His genesis and nurture, on that Screen

All this within ourselves is there declared
And more, a record of it all's preserved.
I care not, much, for Man: tell *all* to Man
(To the most of men) tell nothing; although some few
Strangely *divine*—the Clerk will underline
That word—strangely *divine* (spies that they are)
The whole truth in a tittle. No, it's not Man
We have to beware of but the Adversary.
Our great traducer, Milton—that disguise
The author of our being then put on—
Hid from us this: whatever's on that Screen
Once shown, lapses from show, is "in the Record."

BELIAL:

Are you suggesting, sir, we re-enact
Here, for our own sake, ourselves the audience,
That old, well-studied parable of the Tree?

SATAN:

Re-enact it and re-edit; change the ending.

BELIAL:

Keep in our stations and obey the rules?
Let all the tempting tushery go hang?

Pointing up to the Impending Screen.

I, Belial, become a shrewder Eve!

SATAN:

Exactly. There are those who know themselves
Too well to know what's what. Are you perhaps so?

BELIAL:

I have no answer. I find the question curious.

SATAN:

It will be answered for you. Now, who is it
Would recommend that the Impending Screen should tell?

The FIENDS *look at one another in silence.*

BEELZEBUB:

To quiet these qualms, old hungers that will echo,
Let us return to Faustus. Bear in mind

252

That every view's a view, never the what
We would like to see, but a reverted vision.
To answer Moloch's earlier question, see
Here on our underviewer, here he is,
Our Faustus in his latest meditation
Deep sunk in his reflections

SATAN:
                              This completes
My right hand, here, Beelzebub's report.

Lights spread to FAUSTUS *at his card table as before, and* FIENDS
turn to watch him.

FAUSTUS:
Suppose I know that THEY are listening in,
Observe my thought, as well as note my words.
It's likelier than not—so be they BE,
Aren't merely my own fancy's lively birds.
Plainly, if so, I don't have to begin!

Gets up and comes forward.

I've been on tap (*twists imaginary faucet*), I take it, all my
        life,
"Ever in my great Taskmaster's eye"
Taskmasters, in the plural, though, with me
And I suspect, with Milton too, or why
All that ambition, arrogance, and strife.

"By that sin fell the angels" wrote a greater—
And did not lose it through their fall, alack!
(Modesty would now the more become them)
Who take through me their route to clamber back
By the crack that splits the creature from creator.

Suppose I am some shadowings somehow thrown
Upon this rockhouse barrier, my mind.
(Let be, awhile, the film—whatever throws them—
Let be the light—or lights maybe—behind
Let doubt all doubts of how the show is shown)

With shadows, radiant clearings of lit ground,
Bright as salt, so lit, and pure as snow,
Through which the very grain of the wall can show.
What glint! What crumble! A bit dazzling though—
As the parent cave—in the eyeball here—has found.

You too, old fiends, what are you? What not? Who?
Patches of bright and somber? Not at all!
Initial signs at most initials are,
As ultimate as that the Earth's a ball!
To switch the image, are you planets too?

Half night, half day, a-sway in a seeming void
Stable because a-spin and swinging round,
Lost, desperate, frantic in your tethered flight
About your source, your dance deployed
To bring you ever whither you are bound.

Mocking imaginary FIENDS.

And do you shine in your own right as well?
Give back what you are given, in some measure,
But further, add? Conserve the sum of good,
Enhance it too? Reinvest your treasure?
Fine questions these . . . should tease these Lords of Hell!

Well, come what may, keep up the talk on goals.
And I should win my own share of the fun!
Those fellows think they have it in a hitch.
The question's: Which? and I've another one:
"All things that move between the quiet poles."

FAUSTUS *blacks out. Lights on* FIENDS *as before.*

MAMMON:
Well, Mr. Chairman, if I may say so, this
Is hardly the Report our President
Had led us to expect.

BELIAL:
Perhaps it is.
Not all were optimistic. Didn't Moloch
Raise his unheeded question at the start?
Beelzebub's reply then seemed evasive.
Now, it's plain ominous.

MOLOCH:
In any case,
None can deny now! It's gone past whitewashing!
This instrument, this sound, this speculum,
This crafty, expensive, O so secret product
Of slow contrivance, this high masterpiece
Of managerial art's no good at all.
The upstart worm presumes to mock at us.
Have I the Board's good leave to pash him?

MAMMON:
No!
We yet have uses for him. Mr. Chairman,
Recalling your and Beelzebub's strong pleas
For unity among us, I propose
—As our surest means of healing any breaches—
Wider participation. Moloch, Belial, and I
In this Faustus thing have been mere onlookers
And hardly that: the claims of secrecy
Shut us out uninformed. We've no idea
Of what you have or haven't done to him.
We do agree security forbids
Use of the Impending Screen, though Faustus seems
To have no strings on what he prattles of.
It's clear, though, he's deranged.

BELIAL:
Beyond a doubt!
I hazard the guess that he has been ill used
Too much, too long.

MOLOCH:
Piffle! We've not begun!

MAMMON:

Anyway, it's plain he's out of order.
But since—however, as yet, all's gone astray—
The original plan, agreed on at the start
By all of us in Council at our last . . .

BEELZEBUB:

The last but one.

MAMMON:

Quite right! The General Epochal Meeting
Before the one preceding this—agreed by all
This Faustus should be prepared and lowered
As grating, grid or psycho-spectrograph,
Or what you will, to show what radiations
From that suspected SOURCE (or sources) now
We need watch out for most, then let us still
Go on with him—but with this revision:
That we three, Moloch, Belial, and I
Now put him through our individual tests.

MOLOCH:

I know what test I'd give him!

BELIAL:

So do I!

MAMMON:

Tests circumscribed, devised, and calculated
To bring out one or other character,
Translucence or opacity in his Being.
So, thereafter . . .

BELIAL:

We may the better savor
The use that he can be to us in the project,
Or, that failing . . .

MOLOCH:

Wipe him off the earth.

BEELZEBUB:

A point of order.

SATAN:

Yes, Beelzebub?

BEELZEBUB:

Perhaps a bit pedantic, but hadn't we better
Ask the Clerk to look up the paragraphs in our Charter
Authorizing us to devise and apply such tests?

SOPHIA:

They have already been looked up. It is in order.

SATAN:

Then it's all clear, I take it, President?

BEELZEBUB:

All clear. And may I profit by this chance
To say how happy we are to have such supplements
To our, no doubt, not too well guided efforts
Toward our common aim. I assume that you,
Lord Mammon, will begin the round. Your steps,
No question of it, will greatly extend our knowledge.

MAMMON:

I'll just send down a vehicle of mine
Through which I'll try him out. And—O yes—may I
Have the usual one-way presence on in force?

BEELZEBUB:

Standard exposures: feelings, thoughts, desires,
The lot. You know of course that this direct inspection
Of human minds can only operate
While we ourselves remain invisible
Or use an *undetected* vehicle.
The interference otherwise is too great.
However, among fiends . . .
And may I remind you—I feel like a stewardess
In one of those planes they are so proud to fly in—
Don't leave your private opinions in the open.
While this clairvoyancy Psy-ray field's in action
Whatever any of us may think, our personal feelings
Are more or less on show to all. We've had,

You will remember, one or two incidents,
Embarrassments, indiscretions, awkwardnesses,
I'm sure, we will all prefer to have no more.

BELIAL:

Hadn't we perhaps better . . .

BEELZEBUB:

                Why yes, of course,
Belial reminds me we can take care of this.
As a precaution, no doubt unnecessary,
Here, for each of us we can now provide
New insulators . . .

Subordinate DEMONS *bring Headpieces to* BELIAL *and* BEELZE-
BUB *who hand them to others and help them to put them on.*

BELIAL:

               You slip them on like this.
Now do you notice—I've switched the Psy-rays on—
A mild quietus, lessening of tension . . . ?
Try them off and on, aren't they restful?

MAMMON:

              Most remarkable!

MOLOCH:

               Rockaby, Baby!

SATAN:

Highly convenient!

BEELZEBUB:

            These new screens, of course,
We owe in chief to Belial's special studies.

BELIAL:

For myself I've found them useful. Especially
In observations of the onset of seduction
And analogous enquiries. A later model
Will, I hope, be invisible, undetectable.
Handy when you are feeling charitable
Or merely diplomatic.

BEELZEBUB (*taking mask off*):

             These covers off
We are open to each other. As to Faustus,

We'll see and hear him totally: thought and feelings.
He'll have your visitant, for the rest must guess.

BELIAL:

It's playing somewhat safe. Although I know him
I'd say he hasn't the frailest ghost of a chance.

MOLOCH:

Why we must play any game here's quite beyond me.
Why not make certain quickly while there's time?
What's power for? Use it while you have it.
But, if you *will* make it a gamble, mine's on him.

ACT II

FAUSTUS *as before in his study. Owl hoots.*

FAUSTUS:

Ha! Hark at that! (*Owl hoots twice again fearsomely.*)
                  If I were now my namesake,
Old Doctor Faustus back in Wertenberg,
I'd build a bit on that! (*Gets up and walks about.*)
                  The random creaking
Of these old crazy boards, that crazy bird
(*Owl hoots again.*)
My crazy self that won't take note of omens
Well-omened Faustus won't! (*Owl hoots again.*)

"It was the owl that shriek'd, the fatal bellman
Which gives the stern'st good night."
"They say the owl was a baker's daughter.
Lord, we know what we are, but know not what
We may be!" Dear old Shakespeare! "Any stratagem,
Device, contrivance, practice, ruse, *disguise*"
Disguise . . . No use asking too hard of anyone, "Who are
        you?"
Ask yourself, and what do you get as an answer?
Best take things at face value while you can.

He takes a chair and places it as for a visitor.
Stands looking at the door. A soft knock.
FAUSTUS *nods and holds up a finger. Knock repeated.*

Come in!

Enter good-looking girl, career type, in a very good suit.

MAMMON VEHICLE:

You will forgive me, I hope, Lord Faustus. I've been sent
By the World Population Control Bureau, you know,
To ascertain your views on rationing.

FAUSTUS:

Rationing?

M-V:

Yes, how to allocate their quotas to the nations.

FAUSTUS:

My views! I haven't any. Leave me out.

M-V:

No views! How careless! As great a man as you
Has his responsibilities to the planet.

FAUSTUS:

Responsibilities! A girl like you
Has hers. What's your present line now? How many?

M-V:

I'm not quite sure, Lord Faustus, I understand you.

FAUSTUS:

How many babes will *you* have, that's my question.

M-V:

That, Lord Faustus, is entirely my own concern.
What children I have and when and whose and how
And the rest of it are a private personal matter.

FAUSTUS:

With which Population Control has nothing at all to do?
I doubt it. But, if so, so are my views.

M-V:

I hope, sir, you'll see that that's untenable.
You are a man of the highest possible intelligence.

FAUSTUS:

And what do you think you are?

M-V:

                    Still, for all that . . .

261

FAUSTUS:

You want a story from me on population?

M-V:

The genetics angle with stress on the shortages.

FAUSTUS:

There are other angles. Remember your children may
Have the novel duty of voting for your demise.

The lights switch up to the Watchers.

BELIAL:

Your vehicle, Mammon, though I say it, is pretty smart!

MAMMON:

Thank you, Belial! From you! You ought to know!

BELIAL:

Better watch out, though! Don't forget our aim!
Don't let your succedaneum succumb!

MAMMON:

Ha! Green-eyed are we still, my Belial!

BELIAL:

No! But such tactics can be rather dazzling.

SATAN:

The aim is samplings of the suspect light.

Back to Faustus' study.

FAUSTUS:

Look here! Do you want quantity or quality?

M-V (*writing in her pad*):

"Quantity or quality?"

FAUSTUS:

The question is if you can have them both.

M-V:

"both"

FAUSTUS:

You want them both, of course, if you can get them.

M-V:

And can't you?

262

FAUSTUS:
  Well, but can you? Tell me how.
M-V:
  I should have thought modern technology,
  Automation, novel sources of energy,
  Improved training of operatives,
  Shorter hours, higher efficiency,
  Fuller use of leisure . . .
FAUSTUS:
                    And so on
M-V:
  And so on
FAUSTUS:
                    and on and on and on . . .
M-V:
  Yes
FAUSTUS:
  Would?
M-V:
  Yes
FAUSTUS:
  Would?
M-V:
  Why give us what we want: all of the best.
FAUSTUS:
  You mentioned, or didn't you mention, education?
M-V:
  Training of operatives, fuller use of leisure . . .
FAUSTUS:
  And is that quite the same?
M-V:
                    I don't quite get you.
FAUSTUS:
  It is not what's offered, or what's in supply,
  But what they'll take that matters. That's the curve

To watch. That's the root of econometrics.
Too much may be more deadly than too little.

M-V:

A moral truth indeed! O sir, I'm dazzled!

FAUSTUS:

You might be if you followed it a bit further.
Take yourself now. You've looked into a mirror?
Don't look self-conscious! You have seen your nose.
You know, better than I do, why it's handsome.
Not too much or too little. You've generalized.
You've enough other examples lying handy.
You'd hope to be as just in thought and deed?
Or don't you?

M-V:

I'm here to take your message.

FAUSTUS:

Not here to think? I think you are better than that.

M-V:

I'm not here to talk of me, but for your message.

FAUSTUS:

O simply measure: the law of every craft
The life of the cell.

M-V:

Very inter-esting!
But what has this to do with population?

FAUSTUS:

You don't work that out?

M-V:

You spell it out!

FAUSTUS:

You are up to something. What is it now? Confess!

The lights switch up to the Watchers.

BEELZEBUB:

I thought our man was being a little simple!
He wasn't. He'd begun to smell a rat!

264

MAMMON:

I must say how I relish your choice of phrasing.

BEELZEBUB:

Never mind that. I know it isn't easy
Being two or more people at once, I mean.
All the same, I'm warning you now: Look out!

MOLOCH:

Another damned professor! I don't trust him!
Goody-goody! It's he who'd better look out.

Back to Faustus' study.

FAUSTUS:

Don't be afraid! I'm not trying now to convert you.
He'd be an owl who thought anyone could do that!
No "Come to the Mercy Bench!" about all this!
Straight physiology: the balanced diet.

M-V:

I did hope you'd touch on the genetics.

FAUSTUS:

This is it and I'm wondering why you won't see it.

M-V:

Explain it if you can. I wonder if you can.

FAUSTUS (*as if to himself*):

A test! A challenge!
(*Soliloquy up front*) There's no test ever set
But tests the test along with what it's testing.
True too of the gene set and its setting.
As plants compete for light, food, water,
So peoples struggle for power; within that squeeze
The modes of power develop and what was power
Gives place to what will next be.
                              It's not numbers
Even now that lift a nation; it's not money
(I see you smile); it's not mere energy.
What gives it *rank* is something else again.

M-V:

But what's this *rank?* You've changed your ground again!

FAUSTUS:

I've not. I have to turn you in your socket.

I have to use on you another idea.

You are only feeling the other tongue of the pliers.

M-V:

Rank isn't at all the same sort of thing as power.

FAUSTUS:

You challenged me to explain, but will you let me?

If I were to convince you, would you change your mind?

M-V:

I don't like rank or brass. They don't play fair.

FAUSTUS:

That isn't the game we are in, the game you are playing.

The rank I tell you of is the new form of power.

M-V:

I was told you were good at explaining. Never mind!

FAUSTUS:

I do what I can, but there's always the explainee.

M-V:

All right. Give me up as hopeless? Is that it?

FAUSTUS:

Look. Power to destroy, as you know, destroys itself

When it grows too great. That brings in a new power.

It is that I am calling rank: courage to face

The oncoming and do what has to be done.

Two oncomings: one is the Third World War;

The other the population pressure.

Nations that can reconstruct themselves,

Remodel how they will see it all soon enough,

It is they who deserve a future. They may not get it.

M-V:

Unilateral disarmament! Licenses

For childbirth! How old-hat!

FAUSTUS:

You are in the fashion.

And you know how fashions change.

M-V:

        Your new brand of power
Is a power just to fold up and lie down.
And you call that courage!

FAUSTUS:

        Don't overlook
How hard it must be to do it. Otherwise
There would be more movement on the narrow way.

M-V:

It's against human nature.

FAUSTUS:

        Maybe so,
Against the received models. But it has happened
All through our past that we who were to survive
Climbed up from the water, dropped down from the tree,
Did somehow the very thing that the others couldn't.
It has happened. It's still happening. Look around.
Quantity, I said, or quality. Quantity:
Echo-output of what's past. Quality:
The would-be instauration of a future.

M-V:

I didn't expect to find you so Idealist.

FAUSTUS:

Idealist yourself! You are spoiling for a row.

M-V:

A row with you! I know to whom I'm speaking.

FAUSTUS:

Do you indeed? What's making you so tense?
You are almost breaking the arms off. Spare my chair!

M-V (*standing up*):

I don't know why you are being so cross with me.

FAUSTUS:

I don't *know* either. I'm beginning to think I guess.

M-V:

I said Idealist. Should I have said, "Unworldly"?

FAUSTUS:

Which World might you be having in mind?

M-V:

I didn't know there was that amount of choice?

FAUSTUS:

You've heard the phrase: "the World, the Flesh and the Devil"
How many of these do you take it you're representing?

M-V:

I didn't come here to be insulted.

FAUSTUS:

You are not,
You couldn't be insulted. Why you came,
I've wondered from the start. Now I think I know.

Shift to FIENDS *above.*

BELIAL:

That's torn it, Mammon! From now on this preacher
Knows more than you do about what's going on.

MOLOCH:

I'll solve their population problem for them!

BEELZEBUB (*in delight*):

I fear the new test series isn't quite working out!

SATAN:

Isn't this perhaps the moment for our recess?

FIENDS *disperse leaving* SATAN *alone with* SOPHIA. *He gets up and strolls across to sit at her table. She in anticipation puts a new color of paper in her board and gets ready for dictation.*

SATAN *and* SOPHIA *only, lit at the table.*

SATAN:

A bubble in Time comes drifting by.
I annex it—so (*makes circular gesture with both arms*)
to record an *aide mémoire.*
This Vehicle game—I found it so in the desert—
Fiendishly hard to follow, both for the actors,
And for those who'd like to keep up with the action.

It has to fly on two lines, hover at two levels!
Each act, glance, word, the Vehicle utters
Must do two things: be *it* and be its *maker's*.
No getting out of that—for any of us.
Easy to say to the Vehicle: "Be yourself!"
But if you *are,* what else are you being too?
That is the snag—to use the old slang of the Ark
With *Inspiration,* with every sort of *Possession.*
Be self-possessed indeed! I wouldn't wonder
If that wasn't the release itself to *Expiration,*
Clerk, take a note. My own file only and seal it
As tightly as you can. O, I know it leaks!
All leaks . . . away, I find
As I grow older. Immortal beings age, change anyway.
I am not the Fiend I was. What I mostly do
Is what I've done already: the Bureau works on.
What I need to do—this note, here, for example—
Takes form less swiftly, doesn't come as new. . . .
Clerk, tell me (this is strictly confidential)
Have I dictated any of this before?
What? All of it? Often? Not very often . . . Ah!
I'm glad of that, Sophia. Glad . . . for you
As well. I do admire your calm, your air
Of never conceiving you could be surprised,
As though what happens must be as it is.
But tell me, Truth Itself, this queer word "glad"
That other queer word, "happy," have I picked them up
From overhearing men? Or are they relicts
Of my pre-Christian days? As long ago as that!
Tell me further. Do they mean something?
Do you know what they mean? Could you tell it me?
No, no, I knew you couldn't. The summer cloud
Fast piling up for thunder, flower-bright without,
Within a horror whirl of pumping hail,
Looks lovely. The levin doesn't see it
And, as it speaks, has other things to say.
That thunder flung me down, lives in me still. . . .
But what I had to note was rather this:

We listen, look in, say, on our sample Faustus
Each of us through his several separate channel
The better for two ears, two eyes. Why yes!
But what about two minds? Happy Moloch!
Happy Mammon, single-souled indeed!
Moloch unmoved by any thought of loss,
Mammon moved only by some thought of gain.
Happy Belial, happy-going, helmless, connoisseur of motives,
Adept to finesse and fumble every gust.
Happy even Beelzebub, my successor,
With all his kittle cattle; puffed up, all set
To steer his Ark, shift how he must his sails.
But I, with all my signs transposed, two-minded,
New found, new founding, and new foundering
Who'd use on me one envious syllable?

FIENDS *return to table as before and resume their watch on*
FAUSTUS *and the* MAMMON VEHICLE.

FAUSTUS:

You seem pensive.

M-V:

You'd be so too, if you served those I serve!

FAUSTUS:

I dare say I would. But—please forgive me—aren't you,
I had assumed, a spokesman, mainly a mouthpiece?

M-V:

Mouthpiece, yes! What you, you've never been
To anyone—least of all to a bunch like that!

FAUSTUS:

I'm not very sure here whether I oughtn't to warn you?

M-V:

You needn't. Thanks all the same! Of course they're listening.
Mouthpieces always have mikes now right by their eyeteeth;
Utterly faithful! We've no more double-crossers.

FAUSTUS:

So you are not double-crossing?

M-V:

Not in the least.

FAUSTUS:

I'm afraid I'm slow. Aren't you a bit perplexing?

M-V:

I suppose I am.

FAUSTUS:

Won't they be a bit perplexed?

M-V:

No more perplexed than you are. About the same.

FAUSTUS:

The World Population Control Bureau, I take it,
Are even a queerer body than they sound?

M-V:

Queer far beyond all that! They are an agency,
An organ, vehicle, action-commission
Of the Futurity Foundation itself, no less!

FAUSTUS:

The Futurity Foundation? What on earth, or in Hell, is that?

M-V:

A recent title of a very old institution.

FAUSTUS:

But won't people call it the Futility Foundation?

M-V:

You are not the first and will not be the last,
I hope, to find that crack a comfort.
It was Belial's first, I think, when Beelzebub
Drew up our Charter. We'd been feeling we'd better
Move with the times; modernize our forms a little.
When you first called on us, we were a Monarchy.

FAUSTUS:

And now you are a Foundation?

M-V:

We've been about everything.

FAUSTUS:

Following the fashion?

M-V:

I'd rather say the Market.

FAUSTUS:

You mentioned Belial; and who may I ask are you?

M-V:

You may; you should. Don't be surprised! I'm Mammon.
I've found this outfit rather good for sales.

FAUSTUS:

And what, I wonder, are you trying to sell to me?

M-V:

Briefly, the Millennium. The whole dream packet:
All you want, all you've always wanted, laid on, at will, for all.

FAUSTUS:

"All this and Everest too!" White Hells as well?
The Astronaut's farewells. The eve of battle?
The night before the Eiger Nordwand: iron
For the ironhearted? Is all that included?

M-V:

Whatever's in demand. I leave the detail,
The expertise in peculiarities,
Rather to my skillful colleague, Belial.
On the aspects you have mentioned Moloch can advise.
It's a comprehensive offer, all in one packet:
More than enough of all that it's possible
To hunger for. You'll find it satisfactory.
However many and in whatever ways—
The technical means to feed them are in hand.

FAUSTUS:

I'm really grateful to you for omitting
The general parade of temptations at this point
The full treatment, say, that Mara gave the Buddha,
Brought up to date and all that. I'm not doubting
You are able to deliver what you promise.
Who supervised—with Mulciber to aid him—
The building of Pandemonium can manage this.

MAMMON VEHICLE *bows graciously.*

272

FAUSTUS:

    The thing I am waiting, though, to hear's—the price.

M-V:

    The price! Well said! You are an accountant too!
    And those temptations you've alluded to
    I wouldn't wonder if you mightn't find
    The price rank high among them. Take a good look
    Into this horse's mouth: you'll find it young,
    Livelier than Pegasus and far more heady.

FAUSTUS:

    And the price is?

M-V:

               You know it of old: yourself.

FAUSTUS:

    I know that's in the Letter. What does it mean?

M-V:

    Why, simply, you take over. You direct us.
    You join our Board as Secretary General.
    Salary, what you please. Status—the First.
    Powers?—Unlimited. Yours just to say the word!

FAUSTUS:

    And this you call "the Price"?

M-V:

               And the temptation.
    No wonder that you hesitate. Reflect!
    Reflect again, Lord Faustus! What d'you reflect?

FAUSTUS:

    More than I can recognize. A curious medley.

M-V:

    Plato, as you will well remember, found . . .

FAUSTUS:

    Sole ground for taking office . . .

M-V:

               The belief

FAUSTUS:

    That otherwise an inferior man would take it.

M-V:

So there you are, you see!

FAUSTUS:

Alas! I don't see.
Where's this inferior man, for one thing? And the office?
I don't see any way of handling that.
I've more than a few deeper objections growing.
You see my thoughts. Where's the temptation in this?
Take a good long look down here where thoughts are furnished.
Watching them gather, reckon up this price.

Pause. MAMMON VEHICLE *grows pale.*

FAUSTUS:

Fiends also, I observe, can tremble.

M-V:

Shiver, you mean!

FAUSTUS:

What! Was it cold there?

M-V:

Cold as . . . well, you know. In our old legends . . .

FAUSTUS:

In Milton do you mean?—"the parching air
Burns frore, and cold performs the effect of fire."

M-V:

That's it. You seem to know your Milton!

FAUSTUS:

Why,
I had my motive: where else to study you?
"And in the lowest deep, a lower deep,
Still threatening to devour me, opens wide."
But tell me—now you've looked into my mind—
What else, beside this chill you met with there?
I'm curious whether what you fiends perceive
Exceeds my knowledge, or falls short of it.

M-V:

A fearsome hole . . .

FAUSTUS:

    "Whole" spelt with a *double-u*
I do devoutly trust?

M-V:

                  No, no; a pit
A void, an emptiness, a yawning gulf . . .

FAUSTUS:

It's tired, it's hungry, it has cause to yawn.
It hardly knows yet what it's not set to swallow.

M-V:

Maybe I'd better feed it. Our grand Board
—Forgive the title—its Epochal Meeting's one.

FAUSTUS:

What's an Epochal Meeting?

M-V:

              What would you think?
An occasion when our high Directorate
Covers up its gaffes and flunks in policy
By turning a brand-new page. And that's what you are!
They haven't a shot in the lockers apart from you.
Why don't we two now really start a new Epoch:
Take over and turn the Old Guard out for keeps?

    MAMMON VEHICLE *vanishes suddenly at a blink of lights.*

FAUSTUS:

Vanished so suddenly! It's rather likely
That Beauty's on the carpet—and for cause.
Well, whose turn next? Why shouldn't it be mine?

    FAUSTUS *blacks out.*

Futurity Foundation again. MAMMON *keeps his Insulator on while* BEELZEBUB, MOLOCH, *and* BELIAL *take off their Insulators with bored, contemptuous, irritated gestures.*

BEELZEBUB:

No double-crossing! Ha!

275

MOLOCH:

A rat! A rat

A bloody, stinking rat! Who said who smelt a rat?

BELIAL:

This is what's called "wider participation."

SATAN:

Gentlemen! Companion Lords! My Fellows!
Must I still give you orders? Sirs, be covered!

They put their Insulators back on again, with shrugs and glances, and SATAN *then takes his off.*

SATAN:

Why do you let what you know too well affront you?
Say Brother Mammon here has spilled the beans,
Has been and gone and spilled them—those same beans
Our dear Pythagoras would never stomach.
What's worse for that? Note still, I don't say "better";
Though on Niphates top it was proclaimed
"Evil be thou my Good." It's too much trouble
Having our signs reversed so all the time;
Dante, of course, would have stood me on my head forever;
But that spell never bound: it wasn't valid.
It seems Uprightness is a trait we value.
Our Mammon here, you think is turning cartwheels
A little in his Rhetoric of Action.
Maybe he is. Plato, you will remember,
Plato revealed he means it for the best,
However odd his sense of "best" may seem
To those it would turn turtle. Nevertheless
I represent, I hope, the sense of the meeting
In asking Mammon to give us his explanation
Of what has seemed to some of us more than a bit strange.

BELIAL:

A real question for the Chair.

SATAN:

Certainly, Belial.

BELIAL:

Am I too subtle perhaps in my surmisal
That what has happened wasn't too much a surprise?

SATAN:

To me? No! But, if you are asking
Were Mammon and I in cahoots, the answer is NO
Equally, NO.

BEELZEBUB:

We're all much relieved to hear it.

SATAN:

Odd, isn't it? Our relish for rectitude!
That always gets me. Lord Mammon, you have the floor.

MAMMON:

Mr. Chairman, Fellow Members of the Board,
I don't think I'm betraying any secret,
In stating how deep our grounds of dissatisfaction
With the executive in recent times have been.
The Interests we represent in the Foundation
Have been quite vocal on this point of late:
I am kept, myself—indeed, no doubt, we all are—
Very well informed of infernal views on this.
I happen further to have excellent advices
That on Earth and Elsewhere there's little but derision,
Among those who count, for all our policies—
My Lord Beelzebub, I grieve to say it:
We are not effective. Since we've no direction,
We don't know where we are going, what's our aim.
Meanwhile—whatever Elsewhere may be up to—
Here's Man on Earth making enormous gains
In knowledge and in power every which way.
We contracted to teach him. Yes, and have we taught him?
Why, no! Why not? We haven't a thing to teach.
It is Man who is—no, might be—teaching us
If we were teachable. —"Speak for yourself!"
Hey, Belial, are you thinking? So I do, I do,
Well knowing how little I know; yet I can dilate
Upon the enormity of our ignorance.

277

BELIAL:

A question of language.

SATAN:

If it's necessary.

BELIAL:

Isn't "enormousness" the correcter word?
Doesn't "enormity" in itself imply
Heinousness, or at least some moral blame?

MAMMON:

What's more blameworthy than to neglect to learn
What's needed for our business and can be learned
By those who have a will to it? Who would add, subtract,
Yet not know plus from minus? Would you not blame
That brand of banker? "Enormity" 's my word.

SATAN:

I think Lord Mammon has sustained that point.

BEELZEBUB:

A few observations on the general charge:
In great affairs, affairs truly great enough,
Who does know what he is doing? My Lord Mammon
Within his province, wide and rich indeed,
Does very well to exact exactitude
Accounts, objectives, quantification, weight, and measure,
Order, provision, recognizance, and check:
But actuaries' rules do never equal
The experienced experimenter's expertise.
Long before experiment can be thought of
The as-yet anarchic subject must be sounded,
Exploration must precede examination.
This sound, as we've explained, is this same Faustus.
(Though how the same has still to be determined)
He has changed, will change, as Mammon has insisted,
Who has (may I say) rather the Old School Book
Conception of teaching. We claim we've taught him,
Moloch, Belial, and I, no little.
Mammon too has played his part in this, unknowing.
His Overpopulations, Overproductions, and Depressions,
His Communist demonstrations too

278

Have been most useful. But I should say,
Moloch, with his World Wars One and Two,
His plans and previews and releases on
His World War Three-for-luck; his Gestapo,
His Ogpu, Concentration Camps, and genocides,
His liquidation tentatives, had done
Far more to make our Faustus what he is . . .

MOLOCH:

No harm to hear what others think you are doing!
All this is quantum stuff and slop enough.
My Wars were *wars,* not Sunday School to me.
I took man as he'd take a fly to swat at.
I missed him twice: I want the third time round.

BEELZEBUB:

Now, Moloch, now . . . ! Belial, too, remember
His contributions: psychoanalysis
And its sweet offspring, various and lush.
Juvenile delinquency, publicity,
Advertisement, the cinema, TV;
The automobile as thicket and as toy,
Amusements, diversions, recreations,
Resorts, distractions, tranquilizers, kill-times
Of similar order more than I can mention.
For myself, my efforts have been less conspicuous:
The Examination System, IQ's, tests in general;
Standardizations, radio voices, the packaged market,
Among my many endeavors to encourage
Consistency of demand, the rule of fashion,
The rolling mills of uniformity.
These various measures: terrors, lusts, and sloth,
Now have—or we deceive ourselves—this Faustus
Where he can serve in our design today
Better than the Marlowe or the Goethe models.
Our use for him's severer, the ruggedness
And versatility required far greater.

A word or two now on the high design
Our Brother Mammon says we haven't got.
May I recall our Chairman's pregnant sentence,

Uttered—with a prescience may give us pause
For wonder—just when Mammon muscled in.
"Our aim is samplings of the suspect light."
This Faustus here, New Model, is equipped—
Biologically, ontogenetically,
Psycho-sociologically as well—
With what must fit him to pick up that radiation,
Analyze it, encode, relay it here.
We have him up in orbit, as it were,
Being as we suppose, ourselves, in shadow
Necessarily—though there have been doubts of late.
Earlier designs: Dante and Shelley models,
Didn't work out as we had hoped they might.
The Byron sketch may have had clearer promise;
We've had some other ups and downs. But now
Whether that Light's as dire as has been threatened,
Which bands within its spectrum we must filter
Or grow diseased, or even (some think now) perish,
We've here some chance to learn.

MOLOCH:
     I'd as soon perish
As be asked to pamper that Professor fellow.

BEELZEBUB:
It won't be pampering, I assure you, Moloch.

BELIAL:
If he's as good as all this, had we not better
Start talking with Lord Faustus. He may flop
As heavily as the others. . . .

BEELZEBUB:
Quite right. We may well have to redesign him.

SATAN:
Let us call him then before us.

BEELZEBUB:
      You will notice
You know rather less about him when he's present.
He's hidden from us, as it were, within
The dazzle of our glare.

ACT III

Spotlight on SOPHIA. *Rest in darkness.*

SOPHIA:

Cut was the branch that might . . . that must again
And yet again be bent and torn—until
Rest must renew the wrenching and the strain.

Let Life feed on on Life, Will break on Will;
Faustus must fall. Borne onward in that flight,
He's here uprisen—aloft and rising still

Out of the masking of his current night
Into new course. Regard anew his fall:
Into WHAT falling—though beyond your sight.

To no surmise, to no surprise, I call:
Who can accept a distillate of pain,
Composed, attend a transit in the ALL.

Study as before.

FAUSTUS:

This waiting on and listening for the call
Is a bit wearing—as Marlowe's Faustus found.
How to keep tranquil and not through a pellet.
How keep in mind I really am Hell-bound
And keep these waves from working up at all.

"Abandon hope . . ." What's hope? It springs,
Pope says, "eternal in the human breast."
Who gives it up becomes not-human then?
Pope's wrong. Are not the hopeless most at rest
Though moving others to spread out their wings?

Spread out for what? What wings are for, for flight.
But flight from what? From all the merely known,
From forty years of rambling in a desert
With not one move in all of them its own
Nor yet the drive to ramble on despite.

Hope's suited to the sower and his sown,
Looks for an outcome, tills a plot of land,
Writhes, prone and hissing, spewing out the ash,
Has a forked tongue for turning up the sand
To find for bread the long-expected stone.

Myself as stone: fit apposition found!
The unliving and the livingest at one,
Unteachable alike, incorrigible still:
The stone remains, endures, does what it's done;
The self's at rest and knows itself for ground.

Looks at his watch and stands up.

Tomorrow morning, Faustus! Here it is!

After a moment FAUSTUS *steps forward, holds his arms high up,
then as if caught in a vortex, spins and falls dead.* SATAN *is then
seen, alone, standing waiting. Suddenly he stretches his hands
high, as had* FAUSTUS, *spins as had* FAUSTUS, *but falls into a
formal expectant posture.*
Enter FAUSTUS.

SATAN (*advancing to greet him*):
Very good to have you here, Lord Faustus.
FAUSTUS:
At long last, Doctor Livingstone, I presume:
Satan himself.
SATAN:
            I'm hoping I am myself.
Haven't even you sometimes a trace of wonder,
Under new circumstances—these, let's say—
How anyone ever somehow keeps the same?

FAUSTUS:

How we all of us everlastingly keep the same?
I'm sure I don't. But . . . when have I wanted to?

SATAN:

A man is known by the company he keeps.
Change the company enough—and where will you be?

FAUSTUS:

It's a general problem and immediate too.
General enough problems are with us all the time,
Tick in every heartbeat. At the moment
Perennial problems seem to me extra sharp.

SATAN:

Brilliantly focussed? I couldn't be with you more.
A chance not to be missed. Here, for example,
Mind if I take your advice on a current item?

FAUSTUS:

By all means.

SATAN (*taking up from a table one of Belial's Headpieces*):
Our ingenious Belial—here it is—
Has thought up a thing to help us stay ourselves.
You guessed, right off, we were listening in on you,
Wire-tapping, as it were, on your flow of thought;
Always a delicate operation.

FAUSTUS:

Peeping Tom.

SATAN:

Why, yes. I confess our interrogations
Which used, you know, to be even more rudely done,
Always induce in me a mental blush.
We're supposed, of course, never to feel any shame.

FAUSTUS:

Like a good doctor busy on his job.

SATAN:

You're kind. Yes, science gives the curious quite an out.
Now this thing here
(*holding up the Headpiece*),
they say, this is the answer.

FAUSTUS:

And who may "they" be?

SATAN:

Beelzebub and Belial.

FAUSTUS:

The answer just to what?

SATAN:

To this exposure,
The indecency of having no privacies.
While we were watching you we were all wide open
—These contraptions of his didn't that time work—
Wide open to one another! What a clinic!
I'm not supposed to be squeamish, but all the same . . .

FAUSTUS:

It isn't a pretty sight?

SATAN:

It isn't. So
Our Belial has improved this insulator
Our defense, he says, against the spread of fission
From overindulgence in mutual scrutiny.
A question of screens it is: this Headpiece here
Cuts out, so Belial says, the modulations
On which telepathy travels between fiends. If I switch on
This that we call the Psy-ray—

(Taking up a switch box with a dial on it that clicks.)

FAUSTUS:

Call the what-ray?

SATAN:

The Psy-ray: P . . . S . . . Y for Psychonomy, you know
—Belial says it should be S . . . I . . . G . . . H.
He's tender-minded, at times, is Belial—
Anyway, this Psy-ray is the carrier
On which the telepathy modulations ride.
That's the theory. With this switched on . . .

FAUSTUS:

You see

SATAN:

Everything.

FAUSTUS:

Right through each other?

284

SATAN:

To the bottom:
Through skin and muscle, heart, lungs, bones, guts, lights,
The coiled intestines, the erectile tissue,
Down to the energizers, the depressants too,
For all the mind's contrivings.

FAUSTUS:

So help me Freud!

SATAN:

You're right. It isn't funny.

FAUSTUS:

But I thought
You people had a gift, a taste, for such . . .

SATAN:

In humans, yes, a professional interest;
But in ourselves, well, no. There is a limit.
This Psy-ray thing has gone on getting better,
Like your electron microscopes, you might say.
Or what you used to think your Freud might do.
Or like your other radiation troubles.
We've got a bit on edge with it, brinky maybe,
It's making us dizzy feeling so exposed:
Open and yet blind as an eye turned inside out.
This Headpiece thing is Belial's remedy.

FAUSTUS:

A desperate one, don't you think?

SATAN:

I'm afraid I do.
But just why do you say so?

FAUSTUS:

Put it this way:
If that thing works, you'll be all alone again;
All converse only a colloquy with yourself,
Like a child playing catch against a prison wall,
The key packed up in the ball he's playing with.
Telepathy on, you're at the other extreme:
Giving and getting too much of a God's-eye view.

(*Satan winces.*)

285

Forgive me for using what seems bad language here;
I'm a newcomer, a provincial still.

SATAN:

Put in your way, it's rather a hopeless dilemma.

FAUSTUS:

In this, the Capital of the Hopeless Land!
What surprises me is to find you still so hopeful;
I try to imagine what you are hoping for,
Can you tell me?

SATAN:

                   Can you tell me what is telling?
Without telepathy on, have you ever told a thing?
Full telepathy on, there's no need of telling.

FAUSTUS:

No need, nor even the possibility.

SATAN:

Nor even the possibility? (*Pauses and paces up and down.*)
                                  Why not?

FAUSTUS:

Still going, are you, "to and fro in the earth,
And walking up and down in it"? "Why not?"!
Try it my way: there's something there you see,
And here's a sketch you make of it, a drawing.
It's only drawings we exchange at most.
Telepathy enough gives you the thing itself.

SATAN:

My very thought.

FAUSTUS:

                   And that, even you yourself,
You've only sketches of. And they, worse still.

SATAN:

Get in the way of, distort, confuse, destroy . . .

FAUSTUS:

The thing itself, your very thought itself,
Our very selves being but sketches too.

SATAN:

We're almost now two minds with one single thought.

FAUSTUS:

And that one thought won't let itself be drawn.

286

SATAN:

Won't let itself be drawn? Why not: it's cagey.
But Belial thinks we can fish for it with this.

(*Waving his switch box.*)

FAUSTUS:

I suppose I'm curious. Would I be intruding?

SATAN:

You mean you want the Psy-ray on on ME?

FAUSTUS:

Why not? Come now, Lord Satan, don't be bashful!
It's not the thing when you call in your physician.

SATAN:

I never thought I'd ever feel so shy.

FAUSTUS:

Me in especial, hey?

SATAN:

Superior fiends
Are experienced, have seen a thing or two.

FAUSTUS:

So what you are up against now is my innocence!
I suppose we are sure it couldn't be your own?

SATAN:

Anyway, here's this Headpiece. I slip it on.

(*He does so and holds up the switch box, which clicks as he
turns the switch.*)

I turn the Psy-rays on.

FAUSTUS:

Turn up the thermostat.

SATAN:

You needn't speak. I'm getting now all you have.

(*Mimicking Faustus.*)

"Watch out!" I see you think. I feel your fear,
I get your guess. And you meanwhile? Why, nothing,
But what I say or show, comes through from me.
I'm as well hid as ever. You? You're bare.
You are thinking now

(*mimicking Faustus again*)

287

"Here's a striptease indeed!
Who'd have thought Satan would have been so coy!
When he takes off that headgear? What's he at?
Is that bit of millinery hiding the face of Hell?
Will this be the famous torment, the limitless pain,
The undying horror of the cancerous soul?
To see—become—that worst, knowing what else;
And how, now knowing, go shrivel down into that!"

How was that, Faustus? Did I miss much there?
I see you know I didn't. What do I see beyond?
Why just the Veil as ever, only the Screen.

What's this? You're seeing through it—and I too.
I'm hearing too what you hear. But what's a call?
Like an echo returning is your call its answer?

(*Covers his eyes with his forearm, and turns off the Psy-ray switch with slow loud clicks; takes off the Headpiece.*)

So, maybe that's enough.

FAUSTUS:
                    You couldn't face it.

SATAN: No one can.
You too were wondering how you too could face it.

FAUSTUS:
An echo, a mirror rounding up a circuit?
Circuits of the All, control me now!

SATAN (*as Tempter, slyly offers* FAUSTUS *the Psy-ray switch box.*
        FAUSTUS *takes it and weighs it in his hands*):
Like to take your look?

FAUSTUS (*after fixedly eyeing* SATAN):
                    I've taken it.
I don't now need your Apple. I've eaten it.
Recall anew the rocky floor of Pytho, your direction:
"That rare advice you gave the fool at Delphi."
He's learned *to know himself;* yes, in a measure,
However often he forgets, trims, falsifies,
And, Apple-eager, falls into new error,

As I must now.

(*Satan shudders.*)

Yes, it's my voice you hear;
This is the echo broke through Belial's contraption
And mocked his Headdress off you. This is it.
Who sees, as having seen, the ends of Being:
Whither it moves and where it peters out—
Knows that he's not himself, knows it in his being,
Own being, echo image of that he knows.
You saw what I saw.

SATAN:
Somehow the fiends can't see it;
I don't see it myself apart from you.

FAUSTUS:
We are baffled by the by-products of Being
The less they are the more we spend on them.
We've had to learn . . . are learning: put down now
This new temptation, new distraction by.

(*Slowly laying the Psy-ray switch box down. The lights fade and
come up on* SOPHIA *alone.*)

SOPHIA:
My sober Faustus so has washed his eye;
That eye by which his Satan now must see,
And seeing, fear, seeing both How and Why:
How he's to be and what, for that, must die.

Board Room. FAUSTUS *now seated between* SATAN *and*
BEELZEBUB.

FAUSTUS:
You will concede—it follows—
We, the expendables, we who are short of time,
Live, in another world, another life
From you, you who are not, you who have time
(Ages have made you think so) time to squander.
The short of time, for whom tomorrow
May be a word of doom, a word of glory,

289

May cover up this, this, their one great advantage,
Under a mask of leisure, but still are restless. . . .

SATAN:

Until they find their rest . . . there where Augustine . . .
Don't be surprised! The Devil can quote Scripture
And other texts as well.

FAUSTUS:

Be frivolous!
This colloquy of ours—you at your tempo
I at mine—might last a million or a billion years.

SATAN:

So, in a sense, it has. And even I,
Looking back, can't find fond memory restful.
You're not the *Faust* I used to deal with. You've much changed.

FAUSTUS:

And am changing every hour and ever faster.

SATAN:

We've noticed that and wondered what it means.

FAUSTUS:

An End approaching? The reaching of a Limit?

BELIAL:

Mr. Chairman. I'm loth to interrupt.
Eschatological speculation's edifying,
We'll all, no doubt, agree. Several of us,
However, are yet more anxious to pursue
Lord Faustus further along another line:
Mammon's offer of the Millennium, in brief.
His reply had a hook in it. If I recall,
He had: "more than a few deeper objections growing"
I liked that "growing." (*To* FAUSTUS) May we now enquire
To what these deeper objections have by this time grown?

FAUSTUS:

Why, Belial, certainly—though I'd have thought
You, if ever any thinker, would have known
What a reflective general position here would be.

290

BELIAL:

Maybe; but we are curious to tease it out.

FAUSTUS:

Take care your teazels don't break too many threads.

BELIAL:

Cut through too many knots?

FAUSTUS:

Rub out too much. All you will get's a view,
Merely a view of . . . never the thing you'd view
But a reverted vision. . . .

BELIAL:

     Ho! Ho! Beelzebub!
Where have I heard something like this before!

BEELZEBUB:

It is current doctrine. Let's please keep to the point.

FAUSTUS:

The point comes here: every Utopia,
Millennial dream, and Earthly Paradise
Turns something else when you set out to build it;
Like going to live in a poem and finding it
A Government Regulation when you get there.

BELIAL:

That's what poems are like, not pleasures. Don't tell me
Fruit's not juicy if your mouth waters for it!

FAUSTUS:

You pulp joys down to pleasures.

BELIAL:

       Various words
For the one essential throb of gratification.

FAUSTUS:

Not so; and it's not an intensity scale thing either.

BELIAL:

Mysticism: O what fun!

MAMMON:

      No use arguing
With a man who doesn't know a good thing when he sees one!

SATAN:

Perhaps I can help here? Faustus, I take it,
Has a simple, fundamental, logical point to make;
What you think you want's the shadow of the want.
You don't light up a shadow to see it better.
A gratification is an end to longing:
Not there and wanted; here and no longer wanted.
Simple and to me conclusive. How about it, Faustus?

FAUSTUS:

Too simple. Much. Nothing is here conclusive.
Thing and think aren't so in accord as that:
The answer to thinking's another way to think;
What you find is how to look for another thing.
Mammon and Belial—the trouble is: they're stuck.

SATAN:

Go on hunting the same game, do they?

FAUSTUS:

Forever playing the same old played-out hand.
Talking of teaching, they won't be corrigible,
And they haven't the warrant of Don Quixote or Don Juan.

BELIAL:

The "trouble"—with Belial and Mammon—is
They are stuck! Thank you, Faustus. "Trouble?"
"Trouble" 's a delicate word: benevolent,
Kindly, even a little condescending.
At the risk of seeming too amiable, myself,
Let's say I agree. What then? I'm stuck, so's Mammon?

MAMMON:

Say what you will. You are only talking.

BELIAL:

We are stuck. Let it be so! I'd have you notice
The interesting support our Chairman's offered.
Remarkable! Quite as remarkable
As Faustus' skilled avoidance of all mention
Of those old institutions, Sin and Death:
Our Chairman's truly singular family!
"Trouble," I find a dainty synonym
As decorous as "stuck." Would I be asking

292

Too much of our assured informant here—
To tell us what's our future?

SATAN:
                    Not a whit.
If I urge him, I don't much doubt he'll tell you.
(*Aside to* FAUSTUS)
Your word's stuck in his gizzard. *Stuck* struck home!
I've often wondered how minds of the utmost grace
Can be so tasteless sometimes.

FAUSTUS (*aside to* SATAN):
                    It is excess
Of concern with form that ruins it
Under too swift a pressure. (*To* BELIAL) This takes us back
To Milton.

BEELZEBUB:
            What now of Milton?
We have of late—and may as well admit it—
Found Milton's final cosmogony
Less in accord with Eddington than with Hoyle.

FAUSTUS:
Cosmogony? No. It's his high seriousness,
His conscious zeal that should engage your study,
When his eye's full on the object, like a Gorgon's,
The thing he would be offering stiffens to stone,
Erodes away, decays to sand and rubble;
His decorations—you yourselves for instance—
Are more enduring, you have a life and being,
Yours while you live, not bounded by his wish.
It is the term of this free being you should care for.

MOLOCH:
Ours while we live! The term of our free being!

FAUSTUS:
Why, Moloch, yes. It has its term, its end;
Terms too, if so you would, of free renewal.

MOLOCH:
And what of him? The Torturer, the Tyrant,
The Eternal?

FAUSTUS:

Dead from the start, a tombstone closing
An empty grave, long a memorial,
Now worn to wasting sands.

MOLOCH:

There's nothing there?

FAUSTUS:

And never was. You'd nothing to defeat.

MOLOCH:

So I've been fighting
A figment of that faker Milton, eh?

FAUSTUS:

Agree though that he did you pretty justice,
Gave you good words and used good words about you.

MOLOCH:

Why not? "The strongest and the fiercest Spirit
That fought in Heaven." You say that no one fought?

FAUSTUS:

You did. You fought yourself. He was your image.

MOLOCH:

Man was his image once! Has man gone too?
I took him for the favorite and champion
Of that Almighty Evil we abhorred.

FAUSTUS:

He's been your champion rather, your pet and pupil.
In your real wars, when you made war on man,
You used him on himself. We would forget you.
Now that your tally's lost, how would you care—
Whose care was "with th' Eternal to be deemed
Equal in strength"—with none now left to equal
Care not to be at all? There are ways open!

BELIAL:

I doubt it still: that "that must be our cure;
To be no more; sad cure." How rend from me
"This intellectual being." I know it as
The source of all could rend, or could be rent.
Me too he gave good words, our maker Milton.

"Those thoughts that wander through Eternity";
"Besides what hope the never-ending flight
Of future days may bring." —Note; never-ending!
I grant you he liked Moloch better. Me, he envied.
He wasn't in my class. Faustus is right,
Where Milton most meant, "all was false and hollow."
Worse still, I could recall, if so I cared,
Some things in poorish taste—not taste at all—
He allowed himself to dictate to those daughters.
Forget all that. He made me, Belial,
The Imagination—or at least its spring.
O yes, our architect, ingenious Mammon,
Has some as well, but psychologically . . .

FAUSTUS:

I wondered when you'd come round to mentioning Freud.

BELIAL:

Freud sometimes was my vehicle, sometimes Satan's,
Sometimes Beelzebub's: all very complex.
Don't look too prim: a bad joke's but a joke!
We may have undone one another's work on him
But, you'll admit, we did compose a genius.

FAUSTUS:

A Platonic genius, if you like. Remember Troilus:
"Hark! you are called: some say the Genius so
Cries 'Come!' to him that instantly must die."

BELIAL:

Instantly must die! What's this! What's this!

FAUSTUS:

When Imagination finds its spring of being
Won't it hang there, *stuck* there like Narcissus
Admiring its own workings—involve the lot
Into tangles of the self-same psychostases?

BELIAL:

You may have something. I'm finding Freud a bore
I didn't foresee enough the things they'd do,
His Maenads, in the critics' rumpus room.

295

FAUSTUS:

It goes somewhat further than a freak of fashion.
You've set a pattern: when the instrument
Contents itself through turning on itself,
Like that old candle hung between the mirrors,
A new infinity engenders.

BEELZEBUB:

What need to be
So grimly hard to follow?

FAUSTUS:

Follow you must:
Like climbers on a wintry cliff we cling
With scarce what glues us to it. But this cliff,
Though solid as the sum of things it seem,
Is biscuit thin and brittle. Mammon took
One look within one crack. That rattled him;
You others, tapping here and there, suspect
Enough to take my word for it: with one twist of the mind
I can shoulder out exits for the lot of you.
Once through, you are that. That cold void gulf
Is you; not in it, IT. You're back; you've gone
Back to the matrix: aboriginal murk.
To be reformed or formless, that's your choice!

MAMMON:

I can't see why things can't be left as they are.

FAUSTUS:

You should know why: the movement. There's that moment
Take it or miss. Between "Too soon—Too late"
You dangle your keys to fortune.

MAMMON:

This is all too soon;
Why not wait and watch how the thing develops?

FAUSTUS:

Must I show you my mind again? One more peep,
After that there can be no more showing. Seeing and seen,
Touching and touched, all chance of gain or loss,
All come and gone, all possibilities of being
Fill in between the origin and the end.

Fulfilled, close down! What could be further?
That's true for all of you, but first for Mammon.

SATAN:

And true for you too, surely?

FAUSTUS:

              No, it's not sure—
Companionable though it might well be to think so—
But doom on man weighs heavier than on you,
Vaster his burden of the unfulfilled.
Mammon, here, for example, has not one more thing to do

MAMMON:

No more! What a joke! I'm just beginning!

FAUSTUS:

What makes it seem so is the oncoming end.
When shortages cease there's no point in possessing.

MAMMON:

O, but I want . . . I want . . .

FAUSTUS:

           Want then being master,
Want and be wanting! (MAMMON *vanishes.*)

BELIAL:

             But this is appalling!

BEELZEBUB:

Arbitrary and wanton!

MOLOCH:

           You mean he's there?

FAUSTUS:

Yes, nowhere: unqualifiedly NOT;
Utterly out and absolutely lost.

MOLOCH:

He's had it, has he? Couldn't fight the void,
Well, since there's no one here, it seems, to fight,
Nothing to measure up to, let me go see,
See, try and find . . . (MOLOCH *vanishes.*)

FAUSTUS:

          Nonentity as well.
Where nothing's to be had or won, those two

297

Couldn't continue. Clouds, they were, that formed
Under their due conditions. These gone, dissolved;
No more occasion for them. You others here—
Beelzebub, and Belial, you were
Somewhat more spontaneous, were freer, were . . .

BELIAL:
What's happening to your tenses: "were," "were," "were"?
Are we not present still?

FAUSTUS:
                                    Not altogether:
Part past, part future. Do you not feel your change?
Into the vacancy comes what you couldn't think of,
Could but dream; your dream, whirled inside out,
Back-fronted, white for black—but still your dream—
Comes stalking up upon you, has you now

Taking SATAN *by the shoulder.*

Firm-fisted in its clutch and drives you on
Yours and not yours, its business now its own.
Beelzebub, at last, an administrator—
Capable, cool, indifferent, serviceable,
Policy-free, nonpartisan, and what-all;
Belial, steadily set now on designing
What can remake mankind, as Man his world.

BELIAL:
Ah, flatterer; you know my weaknesses . . .

SATAN (*advancing with* FAUSTUS):
Your dream that's not your dream, nor mine, nor ours,
No longer dream but world, now wrenches us
Out of lost being into other being.
On, out we swing, the whim to be converted
Converted by conversion, turning, turned . . .

SATAN *and* FAUSTUS *vanish. All dark except spotlight on*
SOPHIA, *who rises and comes forward slowly as she speaks.*

SOPHIA:
As once into the Serpent, Satan now
Into a greater is, still eddying, swept:
Possessing and possessed: Faustus as well,

Possessing and possessed, transformed as full,
Coil within coil consultant, in accord,
Now know themselves augmented far beyond
Their either compass, now sudden lifted high
Above designs of either; for this hour
Transcended as transcending—come what may.

Returning soul remembering old battles
Noting who lost, who triumphed, who rose, who fell:
The winner crippled, the abased upswung,
Red dawn's decline, drear sunset victories,
Has felt such chill breath of a new becoming
Compose her blood, engender a new clay.

Hence Satan-Faustus, Faustus-Satan, hence!
Leave Belial and Beelzebub their labors,
You have your journey. Henceforward, two as one,
Cancelled your clashing surnames: Demogorgon,
Quetzalcoatl, Mephostophilis,
Hesper, well-omened Faustus, Lucifer,
Falling as Earth, Sun, Galaxies are falling
Falling whereunto, and through what amaze.
On with your fall within the Unamazed.

JOB'S
COMFORTING

*(The Book of Job, abridged and re-arranged,
and with one single sentence added)*

DRAMATIS PERSONAE

JAHWEH

SATAN

JOB

DINAH

ELIPHAZ

BILDAD

ZOPHAR

SHADDAI

MEMBERS OF THE COURT

MESSENGERS

PROLOGUE

Spoken by Satan

There is a man in the land of Uz, a just and upright man who keeps away from wrong-doing. He has seven sons and three daughters. And he has seven thousand sheep, three thousand camels, five hundred yoke of oxen and five hundred she-asses and very many servants. So this Job is the greatest man in all the East.

His sons come together and give each in turn a feast asking their sisters to feast with them. And after the feasting Job gets up early and offers burnt offerings for them all, saying to himself, "It may be my children have sinned and cursed Jahweh in their hearts." And he does this every time.

ACT I

Scene i. *The Court of Heaven. Enter members of the Court and take their places. They speak in turn verses praising* JAHWEH.

1ST MEMBER: As for me, I will look to Jahweh,
2ND   And put my cause in his hands.
3RD   He does great things, unthinkable;
4TH   Wonders beyond number:
1ST MEMBER: He gives rain upon the Earth.
2ND   And sends waters upon the fields.
3RD   He lifts up high those that are lowly
4TH   And the sorrowing he makes safe.
ALL TOGETHER: Happy is the man Jahweh corrects.

As they conclude, enter JAHWEH. *He is dressed in kingly robes and bears himself with utmost majesty. He seats himself on his throne. Enter* SATAN.

JAHWEH:
Whence cometh thou?

SATAN:
From going to and fro on the earth and walking up and down on it.

JAHWEH:
Have you considered my servant Job? There is no other like him on earth: a just and upright man who keeps away from wrong-doing.

SATAN:
Has not Job good reason? Have you not put a hedge about him and about his house and all that he has? You have blessed the work of his days so that his cattle increase in the land. But now stretch out your hand and touch all that he has and he will curse you to your face.

305

JAHWEH

Behold. He is in your power. But Job himself you must not touch.

Exit SATAN.

Scene ii. JOB's *household.* JOB *seated amid his servants who stand in their places. Except for colors and dress it all looks strangely like the Court of Heaven. Enter, unseen by all,* SATAN. *He stands watching* JOB. *Enter* MESSENGER, *running. He throws himself at* JOB's *feet.*

MESSENGER:

The oxen were ploughing and the asses feeding beside them when the Sabeans came down on them and took them away. And they have killed the servants with the edge of the sword. And I only am alive to tell you.

Enter second MESSENGER, *running.*

2ND MESSENGER:

The fire of God fell from Heaven on the sheep and shepherds and burnt them up. And I only am alive to tell you.

Enter third MESSENGER, *running.*

3RD MESSENGER:

The Chaldeans, three bands of them, have carried off the camels and killed all your camel drivers with the sword. And I only am alive to tell you.

Enter fourth MESSENGER, *running.*

4TH MESSENGER:

Your sons and daughters were eating and drinking wine in their eldest brother's house when a great wind came in from the desert and it took the four corners of the roof so that it fell

upon the young people and they are dead. And I only of the
servants am alive to tell you.

JOB (*rising, rending his robes and kneeling*):
Naked I came into the world.
Naked I will go from it.
Jahweh gave. Jahweh has taken away.

SATAN *comes up to* JOB *watching him.*

Blessed be the name of Jahweh.

SATAN *comes forward and speaks to the audience.*

SATAN:
In all this Job did not sin, or say to God, "Thou fool."

Scene iii. *The Court of Heaven. Enter members,* JAHWEH,
and SATAN *as before.*

1ST MEMBER:	As for me, I will look to Jahweh,
2ND	And put my cause in his hands.
3RD	He does great things, unthinkable;
4TH	Wonders beyond number:
1ST MEMBER:	He gives rain upon the Earth.
2ND	And sends waters upon the fields.
3RD	He lifts up high those that are lowly
4TH	And the sorrowing he makes safe.
ALL TOGETHER:	Happy is the man Jahweh corrects.

JAHWEH:
Whence comest thou?

SATAN:
From going to and fro on the earth and walking up and down
on it.

JAHWEH:
Have you considered my servant Job? There is no other like
him on earth: a just and upright man who keeps away from

307

wrong-doing. He is as he was, though you moved me against him to destroy him without cause.

SATAN:

Skin within skin. All that a man has will he give for his life. Stretch out your hand and touch him himself and he will curse you—to your face.

JAHWEH:

Behold. He is in your power. But do not take his life.

Exit SATAN.

Scene iv. *The town dump.* JOB *seated in the ashes, in rags, scraping himself with a piece of broken pot. Enter* SATAN, *unseen. He goes up to* JOB *and watches him. Enter* DINAH, *Job's wife, with a pot of water on her head. She puts it down near* JOB, *makes up the little fire before him and stands opposite him.*

DINAH:

Will you be absolute for Jahweh yet? Say to him "Thou fool!" and die.

JOB:

You speak as one of the foolish women would. What! Are we to take good from the hand of Jahweh and not take evil?

Exit SATAN.

DINAH *sits down beside* JOB, *putting her arm round him. He continues to scrape himself.*

ACT II

Scene i. *Town dump as before.* JOB *and* DINAH *are sitting by their little fire. Enter* SATAN *unseen by them. He studies them; then beckons. Enter* JAHWEH. *They take up a position together from which they can watch.*

Enter then ELIPHAZ, BILDAD, *and* ZOPHAR, *bearing themselves much in the style of the Three Kings* (*the Magi*). DINAH *rises and bows low in welcome.* JOB *seems hardly to notice them. They seat themselves.* DINAH *sits down again.*

JOB (*slowly rising, then kneeling and looking up to Heaven*):
O that I were as in the months of old,
As in the days when Jahweh watched over me,
When his lamp was upon my head
And by its light I walked through the darkness;
That I were as in my then autumn years
When his friendship was within my house,
When the All-powerful was at my side,
And my children were about me.

DINAH *kneels too and shakes with sorrow.* JAHWEH *and* SATAN *move uneasily.* JOB *stands up to mime lightly the actions he describes.*

When I went through the Gate
To take my seat in the square,
The young men saw me and stepped out of view
The old men rose and stood.
Important men stopped in their talk,
And put their fingers to their lips.
The voices of the nobles were silenced;
Their tongues stuck to the roofs of their mouths.
They looked to me and waited,
Giving all their mind to my counsel.

309

After my words, no one spoke;
My speech dropped upon them.
They waited for me as for the rain.
I sat among them as their chief,
Like a king: one who comforts the mourners.
But now I am laughed at
By men far younger than I
Whose fathers I would not have put with my dogs.
Nameless, base born, outlaws,
Without honor or place in the land.
Now I am a byword to them;
They do not fear to spit in my face.
I am blown away as by a wind;
My nobility gone like a cloud.
I am thrown down in the mud,
Become myself dust and ashes.

JOB *casts himself on his knees, and raises his arms to Heaven.*

I cry to you. You do not answer.

Rises.

I stand up. You pay no attention.
You will hand me over so to death
To the house that waits for all the living.

Yet no one held out his hand
That I did not help in his trouble.
Did I not weep for him whose life was hard?
Did I not sorrow for the poor?

But what is the return from on high to man?
Is it destruction for the wrong-doer?
Loss of all he has for the wicked?

Are not all my ways seen?
And all my steps numbered?
If I have made use of what is false,

Or let others believe what is not true
(O may I be weighed in a just balance,
Jahweh must know all that I have done!).
If my step has turned out of the Way,
And desire has ruled my fingers,
And dirt has stuck to my hands,
Then let others eat what I have sown
And all I planted be rooted out.

I have an agreement with my eyes
As to how they should look upon a girl;
If my heart has gone aside to a woman
And I have waited by my neighbor's door,
Let my wife serve others
And let them take her at their pleasure.

If I have not heard out my people
When they brought complaints to me.
(Did not he who made me make them?);
If I have kept back what they needed from the poor,
Or from a widow the help she could look for
Or eaten what the fatherless hungered for,
If I have let any quake for want of clothing
A poor man without a sheepskin to cover him;
If I have been unjust to the helpless—
Knowing who would be with me in that—
May my arm fall from its socket!

Never have I made gold my hope,
Or kissed my hand to the Sun or Moon,
Being false to Jahweh,
Or hidden my ways from any
As those who fear judgement do.
Or smiled when trouble came
Even to those who hated me,
Letting my tongue sin
Calling down on their lives a curse.

O, that I had one to hear me!

Going up to JAHWEH *and* SATAN, *who are still unseen by him.*

Let the All-powerful state his charge against me,
Written out, I would wear it;
I would put it on my head as a crown;
Like a prince I would come before him
To an accounting of all I have done.

SATAN *rises to stand over* JAHWEH, *looking down on him.*
JAHWEH *hangs his head.* JOB *looks up to Heaven in despair
and returns to sit down again beside* DINAH. *The* THREE
FRIENDS *all through remain unmoving.*

May that day die on which I was born!
And the night which said, "A man child is conceived!"
May that day be darkness!
May God on high not know it!
May no light come to it!
May it count no more among the number of the days!
Because it did not shut the doors of my mother's womb.

Why did I not die before I was born?
For then I should have been at rest,
I should have slept,
Quiet in the grave.
There the wicked give no more trouble,
And the tired-out worker lies down.
There the prisoners are in peace together
And hear no officer's voice.
Great and small are there.
And the slave is free from his master.

Why is light given to the wretched?
Life given where it is bitter?
To those who wait for death that does not come,
Who look for it as for treasure
And are glad to come to their grave?

312

Why is light given when our Way is hidden,
To a man Jahweh has hedged in?

Both JAHWEH *and* SATAN *stir at this and look at one another.*

For what I feared has come upon me.
No rest, no peace, whatever comes.

ELIPHAZ *rises and stands looking down on* JOB. *The five watchers all show new signs of attention.* JOB *himself shows no interest.*

ELIPHAZ:
May we tell you something?
We cannot keep back our thought.
Look, you have taught many
And made many whose knees were feeble stronger,
But now this comes to you, where is your patience?
It touches you and where is your self-control?
That you have feared God, is that no comfort?
And your blameless life, is that no help?
Think now, do the innocent perish?
When are the upright cut off?
As for those who plot in wickedness
And sow trouble, they reap the same.
By the breath of God they perish,
By his anger they are burnt up.

At this JOB *raises his head and stares fixedly at* ELIPHAZ. BILDAD *and* ZOPHAR *nod together in approval.* DINAH *puts her hand gently on* JOB'S *shoulder.* SATAN *looks ironically at* JAHWEH, *who buries his face in his hands.*

Now a thing was secretly brought to me,
A whisper of it was given to my ear
In thoughts from the visions of the night
When deep sleep falls upon men.
Fear came upon me and trembling
Which made even my bones shake.

A breath passed over my face;
The hair of my head stood up.
A form was before my eyes
But its shape I could not make out.
Then a still small voice spoke:
   "Can mortal man be more just than God,
   A man be more pure than his Maker?
   See. He puts no trust even in his servants
   And charges even his angels with error.

At this, SATAN *steps back from* JAHWEH *to turn questioningly, though unobserved, to* ELIPHAZ.

   How much more those who live
   In mud houses built upon the dust.
   Crushed before the moth,
   They die unnoted and without wisdom."

JOB *makes a sudden gesture as if about to speak.*

Call, if you will. Is there any that will answer?
To which of the holy ones will you turn?
Seeing that the fool is destroyed by his own passions.
Wickedness does not spring from the dust
Nor foolishness sprout in the fields.
But man is born to trouble
As the sparks fly upward.

As ELIPHAZ *begins the next verses,* SATAN *holds his index finger up and* JAHWEH *looks miserably at him.*

As for me, I will look to Jahweh,
And put my cause in his hands.
He does great things, unthinkable;
Wonders beyond number:
He gives rain upon the Earth.
And sends waters upon the fields.

He lifts up on high those that are lowly
And the sorrowing he makes safe.
Happy is the man Jahweh corrects.

ELIPHAZ *steps forward toward* JOB *and insistently addresses him.*

Do not shake your head at his instruction.
He wounds but his hands make whole

As he continues, both JOB *and* DINAH *turn more and more toward him in agonized amazement.*

You will know that all is well with your household;
You will look through it and find nothing wrong.
You will know too that your offspring will be like grass.

JOB *and* DINAH *turn from* ELIPHAZ *to look at one another.*

You will come to your grave full of years
As a sheaf comes to the threshing floor in full season.
We have looked into all this. It is so.
Hear it and know it for your good.

JOB *rises, turns his back on* ELIPHAZ *and looks up to Heaven.*

JOB:
O that my wounds might be weighed,
My misery put with them in the scales!
They would be heavier than the sands of the seas.
What wonder if my words are strong?
The arrows of the All-powerful go through me,
My breath drinks up their poison.
His forces are drawn up against me.
O that I might have my request,
That he would give me what I hunger for:
That he would be pleased to crush me.

JAHWEH *convulsively leans forward.*

315

Would let loose his hand and cut me off!
Then should I yet have some comfort
Hardening myself to limitless pain.
How am I strong enough to wait?
As strong as stone, as bronze?
How can I find help within myself?

ELIPHAZ *has sat down again with* BILDAD *and* ZOPHAR. JOB
now turns to the THREE.

Whoever has no kindness for a friend
Gives up his fear of God.
O, my brothers, you are as a stream bed
Dark with ice where the snow hides;
In time of heat, waterless. What is there?
The channels have run dry.
Dry you are now become to me.
You see my misery and are afraid.
Have I said, "Give me what you can,"
"From your wealth offer a bribe for me,"
"Bring me out from my enemies!"
"Ransom me from the hands of cruel men!"?

Tell me, and I will hear you quietly,
What is it you think I have done wrong?
How forceful are words from the upright!
But what would your words be against?
Would you argue against words
When what men say in their despair is for the wind?

JOB *turns away from the* THREE FRIENDS, *who are silently
consulting one another with raised eyebrows and pursed lips.
He crosses to kneel, with uplifted face, near* JAHWEH, *who
crouches again with his head clasped in his hands.* SATAN, *in
leisurely fashion, takes up a position from which he can watch
both* JOB *and* JAHWEH.

Has not man hard service on earth:
His days those of a hired worker

Of a slave hungering for shade?
When I lie down I ask,
"When will day come that I may rise?"
Night-long I turn till morning.

My days are swifter than a shuttle;
They come to their end without hope.
O remember that my life is wind.

My eyes will never again see good.
As clouds are broken up and fade away
So he who goes down to Sheol does not come up,
Nor does his place know him any more.

What is man that you make much of him,
And set your mind upon him,
To punish him morning by morning
And test him hour after hour?
If I sin, what does that do to you,
You Watcher of the hearts of men?
Soon now I lie down in the grave;
Look for me then, for I will not be!

This I know for truth:
No man can be just before God.
If God is pleased to argue with him
Man cannot answer one question in a thousand.
Who has stood up to him and come through?
He moves mountains, gives them no rest,
Turns them over in his anger.
He goes by me and I do not see him.
Who can ask him what he is doing?
How then can I answer him,
Or find words to reason with him?
Though I am right I get no answer.
If I cried out and he answered
I would not believe that he heard my voice.
He crushes me with his storm winds
And will not let me get my breath.

Though I am innocent, my own mouth will condemn me;
Though I am perfect, he twists my words.
I am perfect. What is my life to me?
It is all one. Therefore I say:
He destroys the just as much as the wicked;
He laughs at the trial of the innocent;
The Earth is given into the hands of the wicked.
If this is not he, who is it?

SATAN, *imitating* JOB's *gestures, focuses the question upon*
JAHWEH. ELIPHAZ, BILDAD, *and* ZOPHAR *rise in horror and
come forward to stand around* JOB. *They speak in turn, ve-
hemently and in haste.*

ELIPHAZ:
   Should a man of sense answer without knowledge
   Filling his belly with the east wind?
BILDAD:
   How long will you say these things,
   And the words of your mouth be a great wind?
ZOPHAR:
   Should such a quantity of words go unanswered,
   And a man full of such talk go on his way?
ELIPHAZ:
   You are putting an end to the fear of God.
BILDAD:
   Yes, the lamp of the wicked is put out.
ZOPHAR:
   Do you not know this from of old
   Since man was placed upon the earth:
   That the pride of the wicked is short
   And the joy of the godless but for a moment?
ELIPHAZ:
   Your wickedness tells you what to say.
BILDAD:
   Yes, your own lips are your undoing.
ZOPHAR:
   Why does your heart so carry you away?

ELIPHAZ:

To turn your spirit so against God!

BILDAD:

To let such words come out of your mouth!

ZOPHAR:

Should your empty talk make us be silent?

ELIPHAZ:

Were you the first man to be born?
Brought forth before the hills?
Do you overhear the secret thoughts of God?
What do you know that we do not?

BILDAD:

Can papyrus grow where there is no marsh?
Can reeds flourish where there is no water?
Such are the paths of those that forget God;
The hope of the godless man must perish.

ZOPHAR:

For your wicked words should we not put you to shame?
You say: "I am clean in God's eyes."
O that he would speak out against you;
Know that God does to you far less than you deserve.

ELIPHAZ:

What is man that he can be clean?
Or he that is born of a woman be just?
God puts no trust even in his holy ones.

Here SATAN *shakes his head sadly.*

The heavens themselves are not clean in his sight.
How much less one who is rotten with wrong-doing,
A man who swills down wickedness like water.

JOB:

How long will you torment me?
And break me in pieces with your words?
Many times I have heard such things;
Miserable comforters are you all.

He turns his back upon them and looks upward with out-stretched arms.

319

O that I knew where I might find him,
That I might come up to his throne;
I would lay my case before him,
And learn what he would answer me.
Would he attack me then for all his power?
No. He would give ear to what I say.
There, an upright man could reason with him.
I should have justice forever from my judge.

As he speaks now JOB *moves to and fro seeking.*

But, I go forward; he is not there.
I go backward and I do not see him.
For he well knows what is in me;
If he tried me he would find me guiltless.

Again he addresses Heaven.

Though you know that I am not wicked,
And that there is no way for me out of your hands,
You who made me, why do you now destroy me?
You gave me life and your friendship
And your presence kept my spirit whole.
Yet all the time this was in your heart,
This was what you were waiting to do to me.

Turning back to the THREE FRIENDS.

Have pity on me, pity on me, my friends,
For the hand of God has touched me.
Why do you, like God himself, torment me?
Have you not put your teeth into me enough?
How have you helped him who is helpless?

As God lives, who has taken away my right,
The All-powerful, who has made my soul bitter,
As long as my breath is in me,
His spirit breathing in my nostrils,
My lips will speak nothing false.

Never will I tell you you are right.
Till I die, I will not let go;
I say to you that my cause is just;
I will not give up. While I live I will not change.

O that my words were written,
That with an iron pen they were cut,
And filled in with lead forever
As witness in an adamantine rock.
I know, in my heart, my Defender;
Here on earth I shall see him
With my own eyes, I myself, not another.

At this, JAHWEH, *still unseen, rises and, with* SATAN's *aid, takes off and rends his robe, as* JOB *had done after his first trial. He then goes across to prostrate himself at* JOB's *feet.* JOB *continues throughout gazing with upturned face to the heavens.*

ACT III

Scene as before. JOB *still standing gazing skyward.* JAHWEH
and SATAN *now standing one on each side of* JOB *and gazing—
with increasing attention—skyward too.* DINAH *and the* THREE
FRIENDS *are sitting motionless beside the little fire, whose
smoke is quietly curling up. Suddenly, there is the roar of the
whirlwind. The smoke is scattered.* DINAH *and the* FRIENDS,
and JOB, *crouch down huddled on the ground.* JAHWEH *and*
SATAN *remain standing. In the blaze of lightning and crashing
of thunder* SHADDAI *appears—as grand a disaster image as
can be staged. As he speaks,* SATAN, *from time to time, shrugs
his shoulders, spreading out his open hands.* JAHWEH *shakes
his head sadly.* SHADDAI's *utterance might be amplified. It
maintains a highly sardonic, almost a sarcastic tone.*

SHADDAI:
Who is this who darkens counsel
By words without knowledge?
Gird up now your loins like a man;
I will ask and you will answer.
Tell me, you man of insight,
Where were you when the Earth was founded?
Who, would you say, fixed its bounds?
Who stretched the measuring line?
In what were its bases sunk?
Who set in place its cornerstone,
When the morning stars sang together,
And the Court of Heaven shouted?
Who watched over the birth of the sea
When it burst forth as from a womb?
When clouds were spread to cover it,
And it was cradled in a web of mist;
When I set my limit upon it,
And gave it my doors and bars:

322

Saying, "So far and no further.
Here your proud waves must break."

Have you controlled the morning
Or told the dayspring its place?
Forming it as clay under a seal
And colouring it as with clothing?

Have you gone down to the springs of the sea
Or walked in the unfathomable deep?
Have you discovered the gates of death
Or seen the door-keepers of Sheol?
Have you grasped how wide is the world?
Tell me, if you know everything,
Doubtless you do; were you not born?
So long you have been living on the earth.

Can you bind together the Pleiades
Or undo the belt of Orion?

Is the case against Shaddai given up?
Who would argue with God let him answer.

JOB:

What answers can I give, being of small account?
I place my hand upon my mouth.
Once, twice I have said what I had in mind.
I will not say it again.

SHADDAI:

Do you still call me unjust?
Would you have me be wrong that you may be right?
Have you an arm like my arm;
Can you thunder with a voice like mine?
Put on now your greatness,
Clothe yourself in your glory and power,
Let loose the floods of your anger,
Look on all who are proud and bring them low,
Destroy all those who are uplifted,
Pull down the wicked,
Hide them in the dust together,

Cover them in an unknown grave.

Then I will praise,

Saying that your own right hand can save you!

JOB (*as he speaks, still kneeling, he covers his eyes with the palms of his hands*):

I know that you can do all things;

That no purpose of yours is beyond you.

I have said things that I did not comprehend,

Things too great for my knowledge.

I had heard of you by the hearing of the ear,

But now my eyes have seen you.

When JOB *has spoken,* SATAN *indicates to* JAHWEH *that they should approach* SHADDAI. *As they do so,* SHADDAI *comes to meet them. After a moment of silent confrontation,* JAHWEH *and* SHADDAI *turn to* ELIPHAZ, BILDAD, *and* ZOPHAR, *who humbly kneel with bowed heads before them.* DINAH *kneels too, but with uplifted head.*

SHADDAI:

Our wrath is kindled against you because you have not said of us the thing that is right as Job has.

JAHWEH:

Go now to our servant Job and take seven bulls and seven rams and offer up for yourselves a burnt offering that we do not with you as you deserve, and Job will pray for you and his prayer we will accept. For he has said of us the thing that is right.

SHADDAI:

And so has our servant Dinah.

SATAN (*Comes forward to speak Epilogue*):

Where shall Wisdom be found? And where is the place of understanding?

Surely there is a mine for silver, and a place for gold which they refine.

Iron is taken out of the earth, and brass is molten out of the stone.

Man setteth an end to darkness, and searcheth out to the fur-
   thest bound
The stones of thick darkness and of the shadow of death.
He breaketh open a shaft away from where men sojourn,
He putteth forth his hand upon the flinty rock,
He bindeth the streams that they flow not;
And his eye seeth every precious thing.

But where shall Wisdom be found? And where is the place of
   understanding?
Man knoweth not the price thereof; neither is it found in the
   land of the living.
The deep saith, "It is not in me." And the sea saith, "It is not
   with me."
It cannot be valued with the topaz, with the precious onyx or
   the sapphire.
No mention shall be made of coral or crystal.
The price of Wisdom is above rubies.

Whence then cometh Wisdom? And where is the place of
   understanding?
Seeing it is hid from the eyes of all living?

Destruction and Death say, "We have heard a rumour thereof
   with our ears:
To know what is to be feared is Wisdom;
To keep from ill-doing is understanding."

CURTAIN

EPILOGUE

EPILOGUE

Short poem addressed to spectators by actor at end of play.
—DICTIONARY

"Lost, stolen, strayed."
Hearing such words,
I have been afraid.

I never, I doubt, knew
Anything about my owner;
Though, as others do,
I'ld hold
I'd some clue.

No.
My choice was between absurds
And I was proner
To consult
Some friends
Who spoke within my mind,
Unawed,
Against every cult.

I was told
I would find
These were unscreen'ds,
Might well be fiends
With their own ends
In view.

That could be true.

Either way:
Lost—at sea, overboard;
Stolen—all still to repay;
Strayed—self-betrayed?

December 1970

329